Emma
Hardy
Diaries

Emma Hardy Diaries

edited by Richard H. Taylor

Mid Northumberland Arts Group
and Carcanet New Press
1985

Mid Northumberland Arts Group ISBN 0 904790 21 5
Carcanet New Press ISBN 0 85635 435 X

First published 1985 by
Mid Northumberland Arts Group, Leisure and Publicity Department,
Town Hall, Ashington, Northumberland NE63 8RX
and Carcanet New Press Limited,
208–212 Corn Exchange Buildings, Manchester M4 3BQ

Designed by Sue Richards

Typeset by Tradespools Ltd, Frome
Printed by The Moxon Press, Leeds
Bound by Hunter and Foulis Ltd, Edinburgh

286

Contents

Acknowledgements

The editor and publishers would like to thank the Trustees of the Thomas Hardy Memorial Collection for permission to print the diaries from the Dorset County Museum.

The Mid Northumberland Arts Group is the area arts association for parts of Northumberland. It is sponsored by Wansbeck District Council in association with Northumberland Technical College, administered by the Leisure and Publicity Department of Wansbeck District Council, and grant-aided by Northern Arts.

Preface

I would like to express warm and particular thanks to my friend and colleague Janet Davies for her extensive help with the transcription of these diaries. The project owes much to her painstaking thoroughness and eye for accuracy, not to mention her canny ability to decipher words or phrases that eluded me.

Mid Northumberland Arts Group Publications kindly asked me to edit these diaries; and I am grateful to Julia Steward and the Macmillan Press Ltd for releasing me from a contractual obligation to enable me to do so.

I am grateful to the Trustees of the Thomas Hardy Memorial Collection in the Dorset County Museum and to the Curator, Roger Peers, who has for so many years afforded me every help and courtesy during my visits to the museum to work in the Hardy collections.

My final thanks are due to my wife Pamela, longsuffering in the Hardy cause, who always takes such a lively, cheerful and encouraging interest in my work.

London   R.H.T.
May 1983

Introduction

Emma Lavinia Gifford began to enjoy a vicarious fame after she became the wife of the great novelist Thomas Hardy in 1874. It was not altogether an enviable fame, especially posthumously, when the received opinion of Emma's life-course came to be that she had been a disagreeable snob who, jealous of her husband's talents and disdainful of his social and moral views, gradually became insane. In recent years the unfairness of this glib view has become clear, and the travel diaries reproduced in this volume help us, not without occasional poignancy, towards a more balanced perspective.

The facts of Emma's relationship with Thomas Hardy are straightforward; their results are more complex and include the inspiration by Emma of some of the most beautiful love poems ever written. The elegiac 'Poems of 1912–13', written, Hardy said, as "an expiation" in remorse for his contribution to their later divisions, recapture, under the epigraph "*Veteris vestigia flammae*" ("Ashes of the old fire") from the *Aeneid*, their early love: "I am just the same as when/Our days were a joy, and our paths through flowers."

Thomas Hardy was an assistant architect working on church restoration when he met Emma Gifford on 7 March 1870 at St Juliot Rectory in Cornwall. Emma's sister Helen had married the vicar, the Reverend Caddell Holder, in 1869, and Emma had gone to live with them. Helen and Emma were the daughters of John Attersoll Gifford, a lawyer forced years earlier to relinquish his practice because of bouts of heavy drinking, and Emma was proud of her middle-class origins: "My relatives," she later wrote, "were either clergymen, doctors or in the Army and Navy."[1] She was especially proud of being the niece of Dr Edwin Gifford, Canon of Worcester when he married Hardy and Emma in 1874 and later Archdeacon of London. For Emma, this unchallengeably bourgeois background threw Hardy's working-class roots as the son of a master-mason into sharp relief, and she came to believe that she had married beneath her, a conviction encouraged rather than diminished as Hardy began to be socially lionised. It is no coincidence that one of the most frequently recurrent themes in Hardy's writing is that enshrined in the title of his first and unpublished novel, *The Poor Man and the Lady*.

Yet in 1870 such divisions were swept away by the romantic impress of St Juliot itself and their meeting there. "My life's romance now began," Emma later recalled, adding that "Scarcely any author and his wife could have had a much more romantic meeting."[2] The vigour and excitement of that meeting is confirmed in Emma's recollections and Hardy's lively poem, 'When I Set Out for Lyonnesse': Emma recalls that "lovely Monday evening" when "I was immediately arrested by his familiar appearance, as if I had seen him in a dream," and Hardy's poem tells of his return home with "magic" in his eyes.

Both Emma and Thomas were 29 years of age; he was introspective and laconic in manner while Emma was vital and vigorous, enjoying to the full her musical, artistic and athletic abilities. The 'Poems of 1912–13' record her abundant talents as a horsewoman – "the woman riding high above with bright hair flapping free" – and the places and moments of their idyllic courtship. These poems also describe Hardy's grim pilgrimage 43 years later, in March 1913, following Emma's death on 27 November 1912, back to those courtship scenes, and his realisation that he was going back "For the very last time; for my sand is sinking, / And I shall traverse old love's domain / Never again."

In the intervening years their marriage was probably more conventionally happy, or at least more tolerable, than has often been thought. Emma's early admiration for Hardy as a writer of promise, and her assistance as an amanuensis, suffered no serious rift until *Jude the Obscure* in 1895, in which Hardy's criticisms of the institution of marriage and of the Christianity which was so important to Emma outraged her. She also came to resent the attention so exclusively paid to her famous husband, feeling that her own modest aspirations as a writer were unacceptably cast into shadow, and she naturally resented the attention paid *by* her husband to the succession of young women to whom he was platonically but repeatedly drawn throughout his married life.

The old view of Emma as a snobbish, jealous bigot, however, has been modified by recent biographers, who have shown that the woman who so dramatically re-entered Hardy's imagination as the "ghost-girl-rider" of his elegiac poems had, during almost 40 years of marriage, much to endure from an often difficult and negligent husband. In a brilliant phrase, Robert Gittings says that Emma had "moments of disorganized poetry" to the end of her life. A proper understanding of Emma, the central personality in his life for so many years, is essential if we are to understand Thomas Hardy, and some of her "disorganized poetry" infuses the short manuscript she completed in 1911, the year before her death, published in 1961 under her own title, *Some Recollections*. It is a revealing and often moving document. Its final paragraph begins, after recalling her marriage to Hardy in 1874: "I have had various experiences, interesting some, sad others, since that lovely day, but all showing that an Unseen Power of great benevolence directs my ways." These almost childlike reminiscences are touching in their simplicity of exposition.

Emma Hardy's posthumous reputation was unjustly dulled by Hardy's second wife, Florence. Demonstrably jealous of Emma's memory, Florence was moved to complain to Sydney Cockerell that "all the poems about [Emma] are a fiction but a fiction in which their author has now come to believe,"[3] and she excised some of the evidence of Hardy's old affections from his disguised autobiography, which she edited, from a celebration of Emma's chestnut hair to more signal accounts of her qualities.

A more pernicious rumour was set afloat by Florence when she told Vere Collins that Emma "came from a tainted stock. More than one of her relatives had been in a lunatic asylum"[4]; Robert Gittings has rescued Emma from this allegation, which is simply untrue. Yet Hardy himself had suspected a "lunatic" strain in Emma, which he explores in such poems as 'At the Piano' and 'The Interloper', the latter with its epigraph: "'And I saw the figure and visage of Madness seeking for a home'". Elsewhere Hardy writes of "an unfortunate mental aberration for which [Emma] was not responsible"[5] and "certain painful delusions she suffered from at times"[6]. But madness is too strong a term to characterise what were surely symptoms of fear and insecurity.

The pioneering biography of Emma, published by Denys Kay-Robinson in 1979, would support this view. Kay-Robinson's thesis is that a deep and persistent love united the Hardys and that their division was wrought by each mistakenly assuming the other's emotional defection behind their comparable facades of indifference. Emma was not mad in any certifiable sense but she could be a scatterbrained fool, dressing oddly, chattering inconsequentially, sometimes occupying a different part of their home at Max Gate so that she would not meet her husband, and often showing herself to be unreasonably jealous of Hardy's literary success. But she was also loyal and loving. She was long afraid of losing Hardy's affection and often tried pathetically to retrieve it once she thought she had done so: her derided poetry may have been written with this in mind, evincing a childlike desire to please through achievement comparable in kind to her husband's.

Hardy, appalled by Emma's rejection of his views on religion and marriage, absorbed in his poetry and social life, may have retreated unwillingly from her, his love frustrated by her superficial oddities of behaviour rather than extinct. So his powerful reaction to her death may simply have been an involuntary release of repressed emotions, like those of so many of his fictional heroes. Bertha Newcombe, a friend of the Hardys, summed up Emma in a 1900 letter: "It is pathetic to see how she is struggling against her woes. She . . . is a great bore, but . . . so kind and goodhearted, and one cannot help realising what she must have been to her husband."[7] At the end of her life, Emma would sit at the piano, singing the old songs of their courtship days, but she was relentlessly ignored by her husband. By now she had become what A.C. Benson rather cruelly called "the absurd, inconsequent, puffy, rambling old lady."[8] Only her death alerted Hardy to his omissions: he wrote to Florence Henniker, on 17 July 1914, about the poems that "I wrote just after Emma died, when I looked back at her as she had originally been, and when I felt miserable lest I had not treated her considerately in her latter life. However I shall publish them as the only amends I can make."[9]

After Emma Hardy died, her husband discovered among her papers not only the charming *Some Recollections* but also a series of diaries in which Emma had made uncompromising comments about him. Florence Hardy wrote to Edward Clodd on 16 January 1913 that Hardy was spending "his evenings reading and re-reading voluminous diaries that Mrs. H. has kept from the time of their marriage . . . He reads the comments upon himself – bitter denunciations, beginning about 1891 & continuing until within a day or two of her death."[10] Hardy was gradually able to regard the

abuse as "sheer hallucination in her, poor thing, & not wilful-
ness"[11], but her shafts struck home and before long Hardy
destroyed the diaries.

Emma's other literary remains are less dramatic though still most
interesting: they include a horde of letters, her long short story 'The
Maid on the Shore', and a handful of poems (some privately
published in April 1912 under the title *Alleys*) and religious
reflections (privately published, also in April 1912, under the title
Spaces).[12] In her poems and religious essays, Emma sought to
oppose Hardy's darker views with Christian optimism and a
positive celebration of the details of nature. The result is often naive
and childlike – "Who has not heard, with every bird, / That stirring
trumpet's call / Of the daffodil true (not fashioned anew,) / Nor felt
his heart bound at that magical sound, / Though folded in winter's
pall?" – but there is even here an attractive freshness which also
informs the surviving diaries which are reproduced in the present
volume.

These diaries are all contained in two small pocket notebooks, in
which Emma intersperses notes and thumbnail sketches, some of
which are quite accomplished. The diaries mainly comprise accounts of the Hardys' travels in France (on their honeymoon in
September–October 1874), Holland, the Rhine and the Black Forest
(May–June 1876), Italy (March–April 1887) and Switzerland (June–
July 1897). They make fascinating reading both as the contempor-
aneous record of an unselfconscious Victorian traveller and for the
additional lights and shades that they contribute to our portrait of
the wife of a great novelist. Hardy himself included briefer
recollections of these travels in his disguised autobiography, *The
Life of Thomas Hardy* (originally issued as *The Early Life* and *The
Later Years of Thomas Hardy* over the name of his second wife,
Florence Emily Hardy), though none so perfunctory as his
description of his honeymoon: "a short visit to the Continent – their
first Continental days having been spent at Rouen." (Hardy was
more expansive about the later travels, and cross-references to his
accounts can be found in the notes.)

In these diaries we are given a vivid and lively account of Emma
Hardy's travels. In verbal snapshots Emma records, with an
idiosyncratic vision, details of individuals and places and incidents.
Her vigorous writing is directed by a determined mind, sure in its
views, and this quality consistently holds the reader's interest. But
Emma is also the innocent abroad, finding "Les Latrines Publique
most strange for English eyes & notions", and detailing with laconic
humour the public baths in Aix with their "very numerous & varied
rooms for bathing different parts of the body – knees particularly."

Emma is a typical member of the English middle-classes abroad,
carrying both social and mildly xenophobic prejudices with her:
"The greater number of Parisians – ie the working classes," she
declares boldly during her 1874 honeymoon, "are <u>very</u> short &
<u>small</u> altogether – pigmies in fact – men & women – the old women
very <u>ugly</u> & dark." (Yet a little attention from the owners of her
hotel inspires her to note, no more than three days later: "Very nice
these French people are.") In 1887 she finds "Italian voices not
sweet, the gabble no prettier than any other language" and ten years
later is distressed in Zermatt by Swiss with "very brown faces, &
clothes – dirty all – people & streets & house."

If Emma's encounter with inhabitants of the Continent caused her some degree of cultural shock, in all her wonderment at Paris "so full of strange things, places – shops – people dress – ways", one wonders what reaction her presence induced in them: "Query – Am I a strange-looking person," she asks piquantly, "or merely picturesque in this hat." Emma's bewilderment is both charming and reminiscent of Pooter: "Women sometimes laugh a short laugh as they pass   Men stare . . . look curiously inquisitively . . . Children gape too."

The curious apparition that they saw was, of course, the 33-year-old Emma Hardy on her honeymoon, evidently as overdressed then as she would tend to be in old age. The first diary constitutes the only extensive record of the Hardys' honeymoon tour, which began at the Palace Hotel, Queensway, and with several days at Brighton, where "Tom bathed" in a rough sea. Everything is exciting and fresh for Emma, Brighton's Sunday being "like a Parisian Sunday All enjoyment & gaiety & bands of music & excursionists", though she had surely not yet seen a Parisian Sunday. Describing the difficult channel crossing, Emma laments the "Utter helplessness of us all, contrasted with the stewardess' imperious indifference to the misery around her." By the time of arrival at Rouen, however, Emma's appetite has sufficiently recovered for her to take a closely detailed interest in the menu. Indeed Emma's almost obsessive chronicling, in three of the diaries, of food consumed is perhaps prelusive of the causes of her later corpulence and even the impacted gall-stones which were to prove fatal.

Emma's honeymoon record is almost entirely impersonal. Biographers' hints of the Hardys' sexual difficulties during this tour find no correspondence here, unless it is in the very omission of many personal references to her new husband, as Emma cheerfully sketches and is intrigued by all the details of life in Rouen, Paris and Versailles: the characteristics of French bedrooms, streets ("all the windows are doors") or priests ("whose age can be known by their harshness & closeness of expression, like concealed concentrated wickedness – like liquid become a hard substance"). She has a particularly fond eye for children and cats. Hardy takes his new bride on conventional outings to the Louvre or the Tuileries, but it is typical of this man of macabre imagination, who three years later would voluntarily hold a candle for a doctor cutting open a boy's body for an autopsy, that he should also take her on a honeymoon visit to the Paris Morgue ("Three bodies, middle one pink," Emma notes, "Not offensive but repulsive"). She also visits Balzac's grave at Père la Chaise, plucks an ivy leaf from it and pins it in her diary.

Emma is again seasick on the return channel crossing and is piqued by another stewardess, this time "very good-tempered – but has the same superior way of treating us," and then by the disappointment of London on their return on 1 October 1874: "Dirty London. Very wet." The excitement of their travels is succeeded by a dreary round of house-hunting but Emma's imagination seems to have been devoted to what appear to be preliminary sketches for her long short story, 'The Maid on the Shore.' The diary concludes with an account of a family picnic at Corfe Castle on 13 September 1875, almost a year after Emma's marriage, attended by the Hardys and Thomas's sisters and brother, Kate, Mary and Henry. This seems to have been a jolly occasion (the driver "making wicked witty remarks" and "plenty of jokes" abounding later) which, again contrary to the conventional picture, shows Hardy's relatives accepting Emma into their family.

With admirable frugality, Emma reversed her pocket notebook and began to write, from the back cover inwards, her second travel diary. In May and June 1876 the Hardys travelled through Holland, the Rhine and the Black Forest. Again Emma is seasick during the crossing and again soon describes with relish the next day's breakfast. They move on up the Rhine and to the Black Forest and Emma's journal is as evocative as before of the details of the life, places and people around them. But Emma's exertions begin to get the better of her. At Heidelberg she soon regrets climbing up to the town: "wished I had not. Intensely hot, immensely tired . . . Saw nothing – great fatigue next day"; at Strasbourg she "Felt very ill. Had brandy . . . Very weak & ill. Ulcerated throat – feel as I was either recovering from or going to have a fever." But none of this deters Hardy from pursuing his obsession with the battlefield of Waterloo two days later and marching poor Emma around the area. There had been an altercation at Cologne a week earlier – "T. angry about the brandy flask", which may imply Hardy's lack of sympathy with Emma's recourse to brandy as a remedy – and his intolerance resurfaces the day after the Waterloo pilgrimage: "Today I am still greatly fatigued, & Tom is cross about it." Two days later, at Brussels, he has decided to leave her behind in the hotel, where she disconsolately notes: "Tom is gone to see the picture gallery which was closed yesterday so I have missed it altogether." Yet, for all the incipient irritation with his wife that this implies, the Hardys were on the threshold of what Hardy later regarded as the happiest period of their marriage.

Eleven years later, in 1887, the Hardys companionably embark upon another journey, this time to Italy, and Emma at last enjoys "the novelty of a calm passage." Her chronicle is now even fuller than before, describing their transcontinental travels and fellow passengers with sharp observation. Beneath the surface, however, other tensions simmer: "Tom very vexed. Dyspeptic before & worse now" is the prelude to a series of hints that Hardy may now be the less robust traveller ("Tom is quite wearied out & in his bed", "Tom rather weak" and so forth). He is also a more tetchy one than before ("T.H. cross at finding we are not on Grand Canal") and we learn that on the train from Italy to Paris "Tom & the father of [a family] . . . had an altercation" about seats, in which Emma admits to having taken the father's part against her husband. There is increasing evidence, too, of the couple going their separate ways: "Tom had taken another little stroll by himself", "T.H. got up at 5. & started for Sienna", "Tom is gone out – I rest here being so miserable with a cold." And in Venice Emma pathetically notes: "T.H. has taken letters of Int[roduction] to the ladies – Very disappointing for me – (For the best always)."

Although Emma also suffers (from diarrhoea), takes her quinine, feels occasionally "very used up & rather ill . . . very weak and miserable" and catches a "severe chest cold from too much gondola at night", throughout most of the journey she appears to have enjoyed rude good health. An encounter in Rome provides a comical testimony to this: "Little shoe-black persistent at Forum Sunday morning, broke my umbrella beating him off." But

Emma's latent energies are nowhere more effectively engaged than in her courageous defence of her husband against thieves in Rome on 29 March. Here, however, it is Hardy who gives the fuller account, against Emma's modest summary ("The attack by confederate thieves dreadful fright to me"); Hardy makes it clear that Emma bravely rushed across behind the men and drove them off, but his second wife deleted this passage warmly praising Emma from his disguised autobiography (see note 57).

Hardy was on balance happy enough during his Italian visit, a sure sign being his composition of several poems, and he and Emma combined tourism with socialising. Lucy Baxter, daughter of the Dorset poet William Barnes, and her husband welcome them to their home in Florence, and in Venice they visit, with letters of introduction, the Bronsons and the Curtises, social leaders of the expatriate English and American community. Rome rather oppresses Hardy but in Florence they visit the graves of Keats and Shelley, and Emma draws some graphic verbal pictures: at the monastery of San Marco she sees "Savonarola's face, like Fanny W's wife & still more like George Eliot. A long face, nose, & massive jaw," the haloes in Fra Angelico's painting of the crucifixion strike her as being "exactly like straw hats, put on because they were out of doors", and she grumbles that "old frescoes are horrid entre-nous (Note-book & I)." Of all the diaries this is probably the richest in observations and, in so far as the word is applicable to Emma, in maturity.

By 1897, however, it is Emma's turn to be noticeably more perfunctory in her travel record. Queen Victoria's Diamond Jubilee, and the consequent scarcity of London lodgings, persuaded the Hardys to escape to Switzerland from 15 June to 7 July. Emma's "diary" of this excursion consists of a dozen pages tipped in to the notebook describing their Italian visit a decade earlier. Emma and Thomas had exchanged fire over *Jude the Obscure* two years before and, though their relations were by no means irretrievable, a coolness had by now permeated them. It is not surprising, therefore, again to find entries like "Breakfast & out before T.H. up." Yet even now Emma's companionship is implicit in sympathetic remarks like "T.H. disliked the rain & cold", "I waited for Tom – he toiled up on foot," and in her ministration ("Got medicine, (oil) for T.H.") when she has to record "T.H. not well", as a result of which help she can write later in the day: "T.H. better – we walked out." Indeed Emma and Thomas may have been happier when indulging their old mutual interest in travelling then when entrapped within the gloomy domestic routines of Max Gate.

Again Hardy was productive of various poems and Emma enjoyed with him the beauties of the striking scenery around them by foot and funicular railway. When a "young beautiful gaily attired woman" showed them the castle at Chillon, we may be sure that Hardy, like Emma, noticed her "coquettish manner." At Zermatt on 29 June Hardy decides to undertake his own search for an old gentleman lost on the mountain, and suffers heat exhaustion as a result. In this final diary, these individual vignettes do not compensate for the lack of a more sustained travel narrative.

The charm and openness of these diaries, written at, respectively, the age of 33, 35, 46 and 56, should generate some sympathy towards Hardy's often misunderstood Emma. They are personal in the best sense of almost unconsciously exposing some of her perceptions of the world, and they encourage the reader to feel that, for a moment, he may presume to join the speaker in Hardy's 'After a Journey' in addressing Emma: "Yes; I have re-entered your olden haunts at last;/Through the years, through the dead scenes I have tracked you." What the diaries disclose is a perceptive, if sometimes inconsequent, lady, not without humour, overshadowed by an unusually talented husband, but who on her travels is sufficiently released from the burden of that comparison, and the more insidious pressures of her domestic life with him, to be able to limn vivid pictures of people and places and events, and to achieve (as she does in Venice) some of that desirable calm so often denied by her circumstances: "You are in a planet, where things are managed differently, or you are gone to the bottom of the sea, & this is a phantom city, or you are simply dreaming –".

NOTES

[1]   Robert Gittings and Evelyn Hardy (eds), *Some Recollections by Emma Hardy* (London 1961, rev. ed. 1979) p. 14.

[2]   *Ibid*, pp. 30–1.

[3]   Wilfred Blunt, *Cockerell* (London 1964) p. 223n.

[4]   Letter from Vere Collins to Carl J. Weber, 13 September 1943 (Colby College Library Collection).

[5]   Letter from Hardy to Kate Gifford (Emma's cousin), 23 November 1914, quoted in Henry Gifford, "Thomas Hardy and Emma", *Essays and Studies*, n.s. XIX (1966) 117.

[6]   Letter from Hardy to Florence Henniker, 17 December 1912, in Evelyn Hardy and F.B. Pinion (eds), *One Rare Fair Woman: Thomas Hardy's Letters to Florence Henniker 1893–1922* (London 1972) p. 155.

[7]   Letter from Bertha Newcombe to Mrs Edmund Gosse, 5 March 1900 (Brotherton Library Collection, Leeds).

[8]   Diary of A.C. Benson, 5 September 1912 (Magdalene College, Cambridge); quoted in Michael Millgate, *Thomas Hardy: A Biography* (London 1982) p. 482.

[9]   *One Rare Fair Woman*, p. 163.

[10]   Letter from Florence Hardy to Edward Clodd (Brotherton Library Collection, Leeds).

[11]   Letter from Florence Hardy to Edward Clodd, 30 January 1913 (Brotherton Library Collection, Leeds).

[12]   *Alleys* and *Spaces* were re-published under the title *Poems and Religious Effusions by Emma Lavinia Hardy*, introduced by J.O. Bailey, by J. Stevens Cox at the Toucan Press, Guernsey, in 1966 as No. 29 in the series of *Monographs on the Life, Times and Works of Thomas Hardy*.

Textual Introduction

The four "diaries" are contained in two pocket notebooks.

NOTEBOOK I is a $4\frac{7}{10}''$ × 3″ black cloth-bound pocket notebook without rules. There is a pencil-holder flap on the rear cover and a pocket. The writing throughout is mainly in pencil; the first six lines on the first entry page are written over in ink but this plan is then abandoned. One sketch is in ink and one date later in the notebook is in ink. A small slip of white paper is glued on the front cover reading "Diary [space] 1874"; there is another, illegible, entry below "1874". The first verso and recto are yellow and the following is inscribed on the first recto: "Emma L Hardy / 1874. / [space] West End Cottage. / Swanage." The final verso is inscribed upside-down, as entries are written starting from the back of the notebook, as follows: "Diary of a Journey to / Holland; the Rhine, / Black Forest, &c. / by E.L. Hardy. / 1876." There is pagination on the right-hand pages from page 3 to page 91, and no pagination in the second diary.

NOTEBOOK II is a $6\frac{1}{5}''$ × 4″ black stiff cloth cover pocket notebook with narrow feint and no margin. "CALENDAR FOR 1887." and "CALENDAR FOR 1888." are printed on the inside cover; "HENDERSON'S MERCHANTS' READY RECKONER, / SHOWING THE RELATIVE VALUE OF THE STANDARD WEIGHTS." is printed inside the back cover. There are six loose pages sewn together tipped and glued in at the end of the notebook and headed "Switzerland June 1897". The entries are in pencil throughout apart from the tipped-in pages, which are in black ink. A small slip of white paper is glued on the front cover reading "Diary" at left, "Italy / 1887." in the middle and "Switzd. / 1897." at right. There is no pagination. On the back of the notebook is a fragment of a label, about cabbages.

EDITORIAL PRINCIPLES

1 The aim of the transcription has been to present the text in a readable form. These are casual diaries, written, as most diaries are, without a view to publication; they contain jottings and fugitive notes as well as more extended passages, and Emma Hardy was inconsistent in the manner and form of her notations. No purpose would be served by submitting the diaries to all the scholarly apparatus which would be demanded by a major literary text, or by faithfully reproducing every quirk and obvious

mistake. The textual specialist need not be disappointed, however, since a facsimile of the diaries is reproduced in full.

2   Emma's hand, though usually clear and always firm, is not invariably easy to decipher. Guesses are shown, and defeats are acknowledged, in square brackets. It is often hard to distinguish between a full stop and a dash; I have made an attempt at this but it is often a matter of opinion.

3   Pages in the diaries are, as far as possible, presented as a continuous text. Some spaces have been closed in. Where Emma Hardy has numbered pages, these numbers are omitted. Sometimes the order of writing is slightly changed to preserve continuity (e.g. where Emma has interpolated an unrelated piece of text at the top of a recto page when the sense continues, below this "interruption", from the verso). Interlineations are not identified but are incorporated within the continuous text.

4   Not all Emma's new paragraphs are used. Sometimes there are only two words, or even one word, on a line; unless there appears to be a significant reason for such isolation, the material is usually run on. Emma's spacing is not always respected in the interests of continuous text. It is in any case often difficult to identify clearly where Emma intends a new paragraph to begin since she indents irregularly.

5   Obvious and commonplace spellings are silently corrected, including errant spellings of names. Commonplace errors of punctuation (such as omission or misplacing of apostrophes) are also silently corrected. Ampersands, however, are retained as they appear, as they add an immediacy to Emma Hardy's writing.

6   Mrs Hardy was often indifferent to the comma and full stop. Her punctuation is nevertheless largely retained in this respect, even when the result is a Joycean flow of consciousness (e.g. "She bows curtseys waves her hand at us smiles chatters her apologies places a pail beneath our wash stand"). Sometimes a full stop is used where a comma is needed, and vice versa, and elsewhere the full stop is omitted entirely. To aid the reader, however, capitals are introduced at the beginning of sentences or of new matter, and one extra space is usually left where the sense of the sentence dictates that there should have been a full stop; capitals are also added where a lower case letter follows a full stop in the holograph. Emma's punctuation is therefore not violated but the entries become easier to read.

7   [...] = editorial interpolation. All Emma Hardy's parentheses are rounded to avoid confusion with editorial interpolations.

8   Crossings-out are not recorded unless the deleted word or phrase adds something to the text: on such occasions, these words which have been written and then deleted by Emma Hardy are enclosed within pointed brackets <...>.

9   Footnotes are identified by raised figures.

Further Reading

For further information about Emma Lavinia Hardy, readers may be recommended to refer to Denys Kay-Robinson's readable biography, *The First Mrs Thomas Hardy* (1979), and to *Some Recollections by Emma Hardy*, edited by Robert Gittings and Evelyn Hardy (1961, rev. ed. 1979). Recent biographies of Thomas Hardy which thoroughly explore Hardy's relations with his first wife include Robert Gittings's *Young Thomas Hardy* (1975) and *The Older Hardy* (1978) and Michael Millgate's *Thomas Hardy: A Biography* (1982), which can now be regarded as the standard biography. Hardy's own disguised autobiography is available over the name of his second wife, Florence Emily Hardy, and its two volumes have been combined as *The Life of Thomas Hardy* since 1962; *The Personal Notebooks of Thomas Hardy*, edited by Richard H. Taylor (1978), includes passages about Emma suppressed from the published version of the *Life*. Some of Hardy's surviving letters are published in *'Dearest Emmie': Thomas Hardy's Letters to his First Wife*, edited by Carl J. Weber (1963). Any reader seeking the many poems inspired by Emma should refer to the standard work, *The Complete Poems of Thomas Hardy*, edited by James Gibson (1976), or, if annotation and a commentary is sought, to *Poems of Thomas Hardy: A New Selection*, edited by T.R.M. Creighton (1974).

Diary 1

September 1874–September 1875

*Describing principally the visit to France
(September–October 1874)*

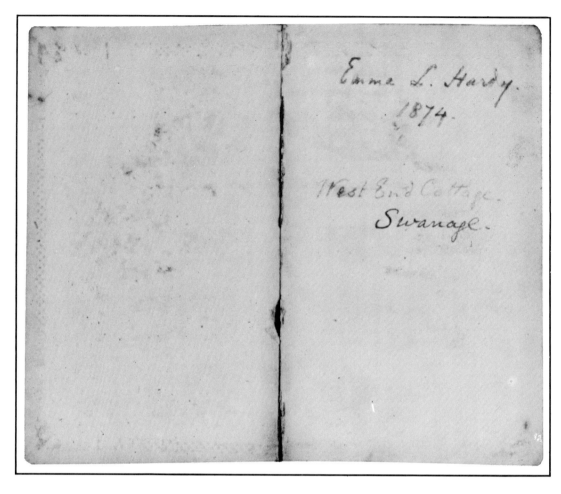

Emma L. Hardy
1874.

West End Cottage.
Swanage.

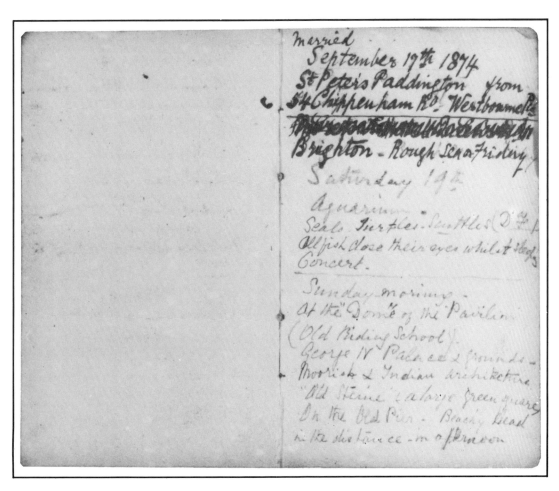

Married

September 17th. 1874

St Peter's Paddington from 54 Chippenham Rd. Westbourne Pk[1]

[*Line heavily scored over here*][2]
Brighton. Rough sea on Friday.[3]
Saturday 19th. Aquarium. Seals, Turtles. Scuttles (D F)   All fish close their eyes whilst sleeping. Concert.

Sunday morning.
At the "Dome" of the "Pavilion" (Old Riding School)   George IV Palace & grounds – Moorish and Indian architecture. "Old Steine (a large green square)   On the Old Pier – Beachy Head in the distance – in afternoon.

Evening St. Peter's crowded but not so much as in the morning. Aquarium again. Spider crabs.   Mullet have 3 claws & walk as well as swim[4]   Turtles swim as well as walk.

Seals' eyes flash extraordinarily as they flounder over in the water. Seals float & swim alternately

Brighton's Sunday is like a Parisian Sunday   All enjoyment & gaiety & bands of music & excursionists   Goat carriages & fat baby boy holding the reins importantly

Aquarium in the evening & music

Monday 21st. Beach – Tom bathed – sea rough. Dinner in a Concert Hall   Dining rooms – Tickets at door

[SKETCH]
Goat carriages – Little waggonettes

Left Brighton in the evening

Collecting tickets of the ladies all "low lying" & crowded on the grounds – a mixture of official harshness & doctor's tenderness Utter helplessness of us all, contrasted with the stewardess' imperious indifference to the misery around her.

Dieppe. White caps. Rouen – Hôtel D'Albion.[5]

Table D'Hôte – Old priest opposite. Little boy drinking a quantity of vin d'ordinaire – $1\frac{1}{2}$ hrs the dinner lasted –

Soup clear nice flavoured gravy with tiny circles & stars & ovals of thickening in it – fried soles – dry from grease. Veal & peas – beef with tiny carrots & tiny onions – quite round on the slice – only 1 slice of any meat brought

The french beans shelled like broad beans brought on a plate alone as a distinct dish –

Then entremets. Little pigeons delicate to a degree & salad eaten with it – little-flavoured-oil, salad –

Then milles feuilles pastry. Plain preserve between layers of puff pastry over & over like leaves –

Then cheese – cream cheese & another Pears & apples served at the same time – one after the other.

Bedroom –

Two window – wall glass between round Table. Two alcove beds & drawers, another bed. Elbow chairs & others – tall bed stands to close <u>all</u> away neatly – Bedroom arranged whilst we were at dinner. Bed clothes turned corner ways backwards   Night dresses laid on bed turned out of bag. 2 <u>large</u> square pillows. Spring mattresses

Ouen Church & the Suisse.

The colouring of the roofs of Chancel & Nave contrasting, French grey & golden buff with dashes of red.

Chambermaid enters our room in the evening not knowing we were there. Sees us writing at our table. She bows curtseys waves her hand at us smiles chatters her apologies places a <u>pail</u> beneath our wash stand. Then <u>spins</u> still smiling & chattering out of the room. Her <u>dress</u> like all the other French servants & <u>labouring</u> class, <u>simple</u> & picturesque – jackets, white cotton mostly over short petticoats – & a white spotless

cap upon her head –
Breakfast – Café au lait   Sugar – in evenly cut squares about 5 or six pieces laid on silver dish or small stand.
[SKETCH]   When a bell rings, a sweet clear voice calls out V'la Museum
[SKETCH]   Carved ivory picture
View from La Flèche de Cathédrale. Perforated steps   Island gorgeously coloured Town violet bue   Pursc 17d$\frac{1}{2}$ –

Restaurant
Vin Bordeaux   Waiter walking about outside under the awning   Trees beyond skirting the roadway, River beyond. Old woman passing along   Short black dress   large blue apron   usual white nightcap

A black cabinet desk counter – marble top – like a platform or stage – velvet seat – girl accountant

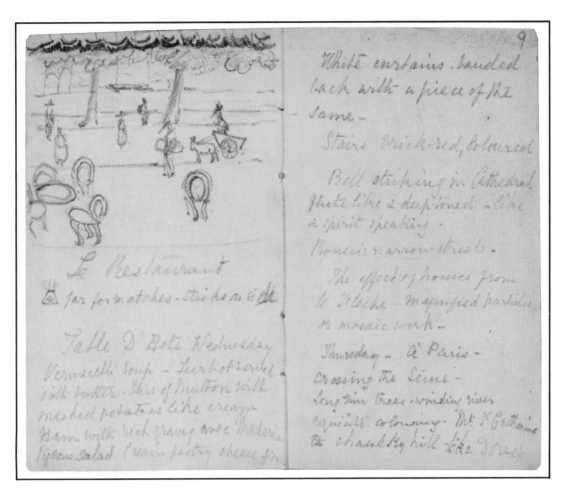

[SKETCH]

Le Restaurant
for matches – strike on side
[SKETCH] Jar

Table D'Hôte   Wednesday
Vermicelli Soup – Turbot served with butter.
Slice of Mutton with mashed potatoes like
cream. Ham with rich gravy avec Madère
Pigeons salad. Cream pastry cheese first

White curtains. Banded back with a piece of
the same – Stairs brick-red, coloured   Bell
striking in Cathedral flute like & deep-toned –
like a spirit speaking   Rouen's narrow streets
– The effect of houses from la Flèche –
magnified particles or mosaic work.

Thursday – À Paris –
Crossing the Seine – Long thin trees – winding river   Exquisite colouring. Mt. St Cath-
erine chalky hill – like Dorset

Women's dresses made of cotton or stuff called "Rouenneries"

Paris 4.30. Thursday 24th   1874   Place de la Concorde first seen by moonlight!
Wagon horses wear bells hung round their necks   White caps & blue blouses still.
Dressing tables – no blinds in French bedrooms   Mirrors, curtains. (bed stand)

(pails) round or oval table in the midst   Men look like butchers – Table d'Hôte.
Soup with vegetables & bread   Stewed fish with one onion   Stewed Rabbit   Mutton in Tomato Sauce   Beef in gravy   Stewed pears. Cheese   Grapes, biscuit –
Stars quite put out by Parisian lamps.

Le Louvre and the Tuileries distinctly French – the streets looking much like London streets except that all the windows are doors – French windows ie & priests walking about whose age can be known by their harshness & closeness of expression, like concealed concentrated wickedness of <their looks> – like liquid become a hard substance. Children sportive & charming in dress & action   Cats superb

Windows all have outside shutters (jalousies)   [SKETCH]
Vaudeville Theatre   "Le pauvre jeune homme"

Drifted like sheep into pens at the stations

[SKETCH]   Gare St Lazare –
Very large station cemented platform – not allowed to walk into waiting rooms until opened –

Sep 26th Versailles
Third class railway carriages mounted by steps above the second –

Sisters – Soeurs de l'Hospice Hats like bats' wings or cats' ears – white chest cóvering

Versailles
Brilliancy of colouring in the scenery round Paris   Scarlet toits – bright green foliage mingled with some September tints. White very white houses. Some with points on the roofs
[SKETCH]   Clearest   atmosphere   lovely woods   gardens   vineyards – Vines trained on short sticks   Drying grounds crowded with whitest clothes   Rows & rows – long fields of them   hung with the greatest regularity in parallel lines   A Viaduct over houses   Bois de Meudon

[SKETCH]   Versailles   Galerie de Batailles View from
Staircase panelled in marble – & balustrades do. Landing – doors gilt round all the panels & bordering in gold. Rest all coloured panelling

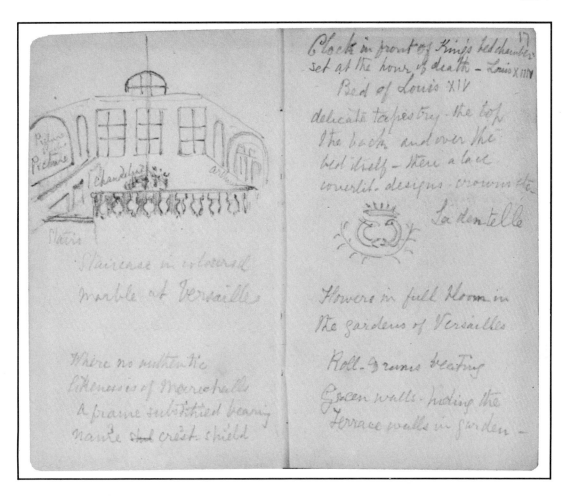

[SKETCH]   Staircase in coloured Marble at Versailles[6]

Where no authentic likenesses of Maréchals a frame substituted bearing name[3] crest[2] shield[1]
[*The raised numbers are Emma Hardy's.*]

Clock in front of King's bedchamber set at the hour of death – Louis XIIIV [*sic*]

Bed of Louis XIV   Delicate tapestry – the top the back and over the bed itself – there a lace coverlet – designs. Crown etc

[SKETCH]   La dentelle

Flowers in full bloom in the gardens of Versailles   Roll. Drums beating   Green walls – hiding the Terrace walls in garden.

Clipped box trees   [SKETCH]

Le petit Trianon
4.5. P.M. Marie Antoinette's garden
[SKETCH]   Opposite a winding lake
Ladies sitting working in the garden.
The little palace about the size of an ordinary villa – a grass plot with borders, then a fountain then another stretch of grass then a pavilion place.

Leaving Le Petit Trianon by La Rue de la Reine   A boulevard – the trees being cut as archways. ie [SKETCH] the branches cut off both sides & allowed to grow where they touch each side –
An immense length & we turned off halfway to Station

Like an English garden beautiful trees etc –
Walked to the Chemin de Fer & stopped to
have vin d'ordinaire like French people –

Back to Paris – beautiful houses & gardens –
Irish man in train

Description of bedroom at Hôtel St. Petersbourg   Square room with two window
draped with crimson curtains & white ones
inside as is usual in France – a wardrobe with
Cheval glass between – a bed with alcove
curtains opposite. The usual French bedstead
in fact. Crimson outside-lined with white.

Marble mantelpiece with pier glass. &
board [SKETCH] covered with crimson
velvet. Gold clock keeping time –

Opposite this a couch & easy chair

Oval table in the

middle – Commode standing near bedstead. Washing stand behind. Pail – earthenware with basketwork handle – Pan with water besides the jug –

At the Station   Two Officers with silver helmets walking up & down the platform –
    Notre Dame

All richly coloured windows in the chancel   Chapels behind the altar at one end & baptism taking place in the Chapel of John the Baptist   Coloured statuary all round the place where the service is held.
    La Morgue   Three bodies – middle one pink – Their clothes hanging above them. Not offensive but repulsive.

Hôtel Cluny   Dark massive place. Heavy windows & doorways richly carved staircases fireplaces. Exquisite carved cabinets – one opened by the official. There he keeps his drinks. He poured some out & drank it then. Chapel – next to the princess bedchamber. One colour spreading like a palm tree & forming the roof – [SKETCH]
Circular window – two little ones on each side higher up. Carved stalls south – stall: chairs. Roman bath place rows of heads in the bath – & other stone carvings.

Gardens & statuary   All close to the street

Père-Lachaise
The street all shops for selling immortelles crosses etc. All colours especially white & black bead ones. Tomb Sir Sydney Smith[7] Tomb of Abelard & Héloïse[8] Tomb of Balzac[9] – Women carry several wreaths on their arms & a can of water in their hands to the tombs   Everyone carrying them

Tombs everywhere strung with them Some having glass shelters for them. A[SKETCH]   Glass roof over wreaths
The paths strewed with old dead flowers pieces & bits of bead circles.
The tombs standing like houses, overlook the street of the living   No high wall concealing   From here where I am resting – I can

see the city of the dead   The rows of tomb-houses looking upon the streets full of people & omnibuses –

This Sunday 4.30 – La Père-Lachaise is full   This omnibus place is full. Our tickets are 140 141   The 'bus stops. But we cannot get into it

The conductor is calling out the numbers of the tickets – 20 something   We rush out – useless   Wait for the next –

Bureau d'Omnibus

A small square room   Seats all round   A door at side for ladies   A man at a desk at which you get circular tickets – The next omnibus is marked "complete"   Drives off

The greater number of Parisians – ie the working classes are <u>very</u> short & <u>small</u> altogether – pigmies in fact – men & women – the old women very <u>ugly</u> & dark – <u>very</u> fierce in the poorest streets

Sunday night   a thunderstorm   Morning T gone out   Cat at the Hôtel Magnifique   Sitting in the courtyard

Description of Courtyard

Brown and white awning at one side – Cane bottomed iron seats on the drawing room side   Little office rooms opposite   little tables about [SKETCH]   Two larger tables ordinary ones under the awning – boxes – long ones – full of shrubs between the seats & offices – In the middle at the end against a wall an ornamental water place [SKETCH]   with a tap.

Sunday coming out of Notre Dame I pur-
chased a tiny crucifix & a carved oval boite – at
the door – There were some rather large
crucifixes in pearl with silver edgings prices
8.Fr –
Notre Dame from River side – the prettiest
view –
  The priests passed almost touching us into
the Sacristie.

Monday 28th. Sep – Tomb of Napoleon I. A
circular marble well. You lean on the edge &
look down upon a chocolate-coloured sarco-
phagus
[SKETCH]   Flags taken by Napoleon

A circle of laurel leaves – green with purple bindings at intervals.

Then a yellow gloria radiating [SKETCH]

On first entering l'Eglise you are struck with the high altar – with twisted serpentine pillars [SKETCH] immensely high – & exquisitely shining – blazing impact with merely the common daylight shining through coloured windows   The effect most startling [SKETCH]   Dome outside

All glittering in gilt   Underneath this Dome is the Tomb –

gorgeous marbles especially pavements
Pavement at Versailles and Tomb of Napo-
leon superb. Designs in marble on the floor –
L'Eglise of the Hôtel des Invalides behind the
altar – & to be seen through the iron gates –
Very small babies in Paris   Gardens of Les
Invalides   Bonnes & babies – Wrote to St.

Juliot in the evening[10] –

Flowers very plentiful in Paris – violets sold
everywhere   Plants mostly in bloom   Geraniums veronicas dahlias fuschias – (Sepr.)
Chrysanthemums – Coleuses & foliage plants
in flower – red

spiral flowers –

Wherever I go, whoever I pass – at whatever
time daytime or by night – the people gaze at
me as much or more than I at them & their
beautiful city – so full of strange things, places
– shops – people dress – ways – Query – Am
I a <u>strange-looking</u> person – or merely picturesque in this hat – Women sometimes
laugh a short laugh as they pass. Men stare –
some stand – some look back or turn, look
over their shoulders – look curiously inquisitively – some <admiringly> tenderly without my being mistaken – they do <u>in</u> a French
manner

As it is remarkable I note it –
Children gape too –

Garden of the Tuileries – Sep 29 – 1874
Little birds dusting themselves around my seat. (A semi circular stone one) Borderings of ivy The new fresh green young leaves a pretty contrast with the dark old ones – These borderings all round the flower borders The birds rejoice in them Vases & Statuary everywhere – The palace of the Tuileries faces this seat greatly damaged – Workmen are busy making repairs – The sound of their tools mingles with that of the carriages & voices in the streets & the little birds chirping – It rains softly just a little –

T. has left me for 20 m. to get his coat – because of his cold – Three hommes

Scaffolding along one side of the Tuileries –
You can see daylight through many of the
window   [SKETCH]
   Tuileries –
It looks rather a dull building – & now tells
what a French mob can effect – A large
portion is gone altogether – & it stands at
present like a monument of the "rage of the
heathen" and a "vain thing" vain to build &
vain to destroy – pulling down & building up
in Paris goes on just the same, for all the
politics & opinions in the world, only pro-
duces buildings of some sort or another in
some place or other – The appearance of the
Tuileries is that of having been <u>much</u> burnt.

A large basin & fountain & statues & boxes painted light green   [SKETCH]   Then a very wide avenue. Hundreds of people walking to & from L'Arc de l'Etoile – (De Triomphe) Mostly children playing <u>wildly</u> all about under the trees on the <u>gravel</u> – When the clouds are full grey, announcing rain shortly Paris shows <u>Whitest</u> – but moonlight is best – as when we first saw Paris – Little children wear pinafores loose with collared pieces – Boy sailing boats in (Bible) <u>Seas</u>. Heavy cups & glasses in Paris – the <u>cups</u> at the Hotel monstrously thick & weighty – The head waiter at hotel St. Petersbourg is a German & speaks 6 or 7 languages

He makes up petit-dishes for the landlord.
[SKETCH]   long oval dishes used for butter or anything else   He made 4 of these long dishes for the landlord's breakfast of whites & yokes of eggs chopped & put in between green parsley or something – & long slices of sardines placed lengthways – diagonally on them, he placed <u>tiny</u> ○ circles of carrots   He placed them with small implements upon the fish –

In the Seine –   Boat on Seine   Three figures two men & boy 2 lights blue   the 3rd. light dull green – charming bit of colour. Bathing houses along the banks – fine places

Bathing schools – Men fishing – but no fish to be seen – doubtful success – Lots of steamers pass by full of people – La Morgue – with three open window-places with shutters open outward very high up – Men carry liquids in tin things behind on their backs & the taps come in front with pewter cups

By omnibus tramway to Saint Cloud – by the borders of the Seine Rows of trees – 5 or 6 & seats as usual – Tomb of Napoleon at a little distance off –

Pass over the Seine
Sèvres – Island   St Cloud – Through gates – Through woods. Come into the town or just a little part of it

Before the gates leading to the Château – We are not allowed within – so gaze through the gates at a mere "shell" of a palace. Then look down upon barracks, where les soldats are exercising   Then go through the wood – up very steep slopes – (after passing again the cascade) to the high ground where stood – Diogenes' Lantern – A splendid view of Paris – then down over slopes & over viaducts (which pass over the lower paths) through the two iron gates & into the town – get into a tramway omnibus back to la Place de Concorde

Very clean streets & plenty of water – & cleaning going on –

Rain always comes by a thunderstorm in Paris during the night – one fancies so.

Le Lazarre station
Wednesday Sep 30 1874
Adieu to Paris – Charmante ville
Adieu to the Boulevards. To the gay shops –
To the "gens" sitting in the streets   To the
vivants enfants   To the white caps of the
femmes   To the river & its boats   To the
clear atmosphere & billiant colourings

Going to Rouen again on our return
Journey by the 8 / P.M. / train
Flower shops of Paris strikingly beautiful
"Location de fleur – pour les bals"   Huge
bouquets of roses with a white flower – a
spray like May blossom. Faces you – Numerous bouquets. & bundles of flowers thrown
together also

Women all wear ornaments – even the humble plainly attired ones – have earrings & rings & crosses though the white cap of the nation only is upon their heads –

These caps are some very costly – or appear so – because Valenciennes Lace is so much used.   [SKETCH]   So strange to have about half a dozen white cap women in an omnibus with one –

The fountains played to day in Place de la Concorde

The Master & Mistress came to the door of Hotel & wished us "Bon Voyage" – & said many pleasant things in the French &

bowed us off – Very nice these French people are – Extremely <u>hot</u> here in Paris – Les Latrines Publiques most strange for English eyes & notions –

Near the Grand Opera house is a Café extending two sides of the Rue des Capucins – and though so long – it is all occupied with gentlemen sitting drinking wine & chatting

The boulevards have two pavements – The white coats of the waiters at some of the cafés. Blossom white – wonderfully pure & clean & smoothly starched & ironed.

Rolls carried by old women – long dark ones –
[SKETCH]
Children lively on their legs – Ironing shops very singular   Several women working – Then they place the finished articles in the window as they get done & before sending them to their owners.

As we walked up the slopes to "Diogenes' Lantern" I looked back at the Château – Very pretty view of it – Stands in the centre of the rising ground which we were upon – grass very green. Trees a-dripping – just been a heavy thunder shower   Two gens d'arms walking up at the right of us & behind their red trousers, & blue upper dress – very charming contrast & suitable figures, in such a place

One room – a gallery in the Louvre – wonderful gold decorations – magnificent room   An artist's picture of it superb.

61

In the Steam boat –

One lady has just come in – & is chatting so much – she has awoke all the other ladies – She is speaking of her travels – has been journeying for a week past – She says she had a champagne dinner – & has just been eating as much bread & butter as she can see – & drinking brandy as much as she can get down – A lady asks her if she is not tired – She replies no she feels as lively as a moth! It appears so – for she continues in a buzzing way about her travels – Been within 10,000 feet of Mont Blanc's summit. The guide fell through a crevasse & a Mr. Marshall fell upon him. A very stout man – his head struck the guide & with the blow killed himself – the guide wedged in at the lowest & narrow part of the crevasses for 4 hours –

Her husband she refers to incessantly much to the amusement of my two chatty vis-à-vis above me – towards my feet

She thinks it does not matter about lost

trains, or losing times etc – for after travelling abroad you get into a "preciosa" sort of life –

The word sounded <thus> – & Calais she pronounced Callis

The guide cut steps as they pass – Just come from Geneva. Her husband says that she looks "ridiculously well" –

This stewardess is very portly & very good-tempered – but has the same superior way of treating us – marshals us about & talks commandingly & independently of how she shall manage us

when we get sick   She shall not hurry herself
– She says – & if we have patience she will
attend to us all –

2.10 P.M.
Rather rough passage – all very ill towards
day-break – When I moved to go upon deck –
found myself ill too – after a while got on
deck –

Thursday Oct – 1 – 1874

Arrived at London – Dirty London. Very
wet –

Friday morning. Drive to Waterloo station
for Wimbledon   Met Mrs Rousehill –

Sunday 4th
"Freeman's Arms" – Wimbledon – very wet –
raining perseveringly   A pretty drawing
room – view – long stretch of green –
clumps [SKETCH]   of trees in the distance[11]

Yesterday – Saturday
Walked about Wimbledon. Called at Denmark Hill – House to be let furnished therefore cannot have apartments –

Mrs Bishop – with whom we drank tea Friday evening – our first day at Wimbledon – says one little village (I forget where) produced apparently nothing but ducks & children I think this may be well said of almost all small Cornish parishes –

The lady on the highest berth in the Steamboat on our return voyage – opposite me – had firm flesh & complexion which can only belong to high-fed & comfortably-living people. The combination grand. In her chemise she was a perfect Juno. Flesh, tinted – neither dark nor yellow white – perfect flesh & form –

<"Merry Maidens"   "Merry Maidens"
Village Maidens   "Maids in moods"
"Moods in men"   Joceline   "Juno on
Earth"   Venus embodied

Poppy Chard or Penny Knowle   Philomel
– Meet at a well   Quarryman – Pebble,
Swiffle   Hall of Hollowholt – Syn Him
[*illegible*] stilt>[12]

Tuesday 6th. Oct 1874

St. David's Villa – Surbiton 5 P.M. Annie
& the Retriever playing in the garden with
Papa –[13]

Monday March 22nd 1875
18 Newton Road. Westbourne Grove. London[14]

Monday July 12. Left London for Bournemouth[15]

Thursday 15. Came to Swanage[16]
Friday. West End Cottage[17]

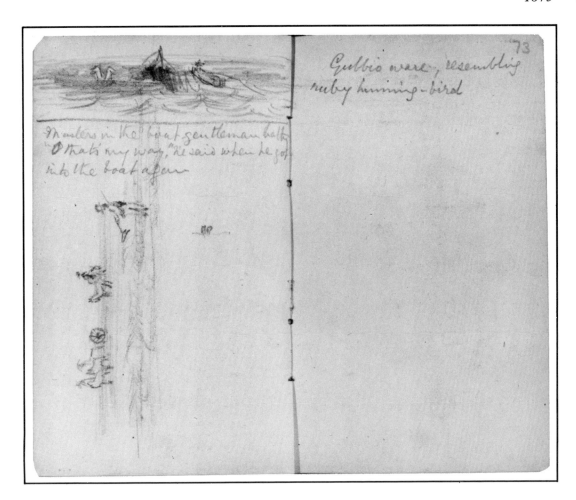

[SKETCH]
Masters[18] in the boat – gentleman bathing
"O that's my way," he said when he got into
the boat again
[SKETCH]

Gubbio ware, resembling ruby humming-
bird

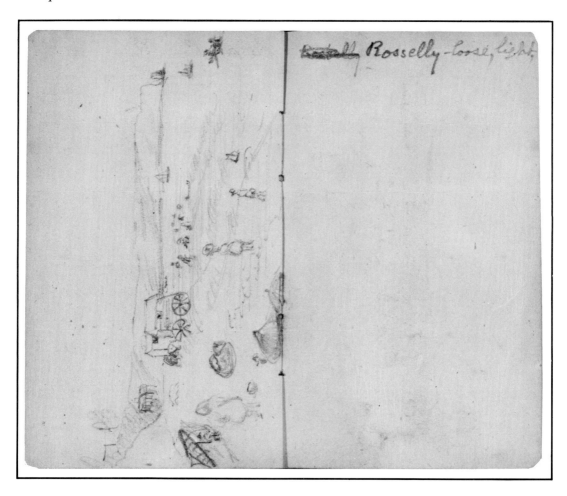

[SKETCH]

Rosselly [*sic*] – loose, light,

She walked up the hill behind her house, beside the road was a down. An upheaved tract of land edged by cliff & shore & the ocean, in times centuries before, it had been famous marble quarries – now one or two houses <almost handsome> stood scattered about in various positions commanding views either of a stretch of the channel or the blue bay which was at times clear brushed of its flock of small masts & usual craft –[19]

One of the houses had an older aspect, excepting that early in the present season

[SKETCH]

the whole of its small front had been turned
into bay windows – [*illegible*] behind it rose a
mound high as itself – An infant boy opened
the gate for her swinging all his strength to
keep it its width open

. . . .

Mr. A led her down the stone steps – telling
her how that this cave was more extensive
than even he had full knowledge of, he had
heard it had an opening on the shore, but that
lately some huge pieces of rock had slipped
from the cliff & almost entirely closed the

entrance but that he had never himself ventured further investigation than he would now show her. For some yards – before her it was in use as a cellar – but beyond the first columns there was nothing but darkness. He carried in his hand a tiny glass lantern.

. . . .

The land to the north west was in working-pits in all directions – their open mouths festooned with ferns & flowers (July) the blackness of the depth showing each spray with distinction

. . . .

Steps & wheel mark

This morning the men are in the street talking in groups. The quarries are neglected. Mr. R. has bought the land & has raised the rent of the quarries. Five women went to meet the steamer – but he came by land to Wareham & got safely home

Hotel, Victoria – Poole – Young man drowned woman nearly.

Church – Tower built & man dies – All men do who build towers

[SKETCH]

The moon rose red gold out of the sea dropping as she trod the sky her gemmed scarf band unrolled her pearl robe which shook its gems on the dull blue waters, which lay its length & breadth across till it touched our shore.

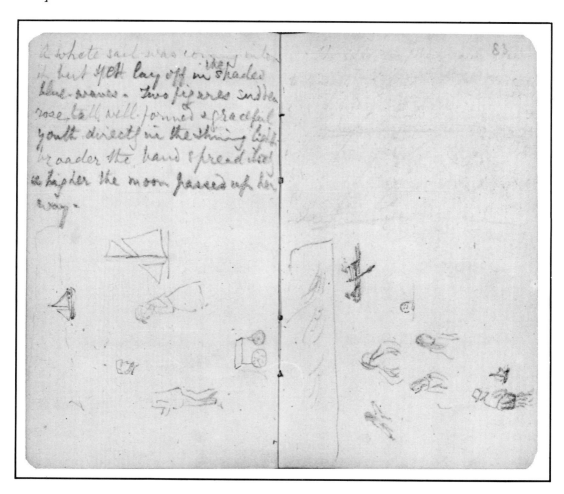

A white sail was coming into it but yet lay off   [SKETCH]
in the shaded blue waves. Two figures sudden
rose tall well–formed & graceful youth dir-   [SKETCH]
ectly in the shining light broader the band
spread itself & higher the moon passed up her
way.

"Dismal conversation is very disagreeable
Why?
Because one is not accustomed to the words as they flow & it is not easy to make sense of them.
"Canary". Make you [dance?] P.189   Dis
Each feature had its due proportion of flesh.

Knitting wool – Crewel

Sep.7.[20] Left Swanage at 9.A.M. in the "Heather Bell" Steamer. For the Isle of Wight. Weather exceeding fine & a very warm sun all day. Stopped at Bournemouth & took up a number of people. We sat on the bridge & it seemed like driving. Invalid & sister just below. Felt sea-sick   Came to the Aft of the vessel, Then up on the bridge. We then passed the Needles   All eyes gaze. Sea rough. I made sketch. The Island most beautiful now. The Cliffs like well-built walls so regular [SKETCH] Ventnor partly in a chine. Many houses are scattered on the tops of the cliffs. It looked shut away from the rest of the world & it was strange to think a line of railway was near. It was like a town for gulls & sea things afterwards – the island had a greener appearance, more habitable all on

to Ryde, which almost looks like a city. A splendid pier with awnings & a thoroughly good band – hundreds of people – The steamer only stopped half an hour so we did not land – but eat our luncheon sitting up again on the bridge & heard the band – The people quietly came on again – Saw a cigar ship iron-[clads?] etc – Osborne – wooded & beautiful – Cowes – Solent is crowded with craft – The whole voyage was 100 miles – very wide across the Solent – passed by the Spot where the Royal George went down – Spithead – not so many masts as I expected – Landed the Bournemouth people with difficulty owing to a high tide   Moonlight home from B. Quite low in the sky, seeming to rest on B. Downs

[SKETCH]

<The Milliner & Dressmaker & Warehouse-man's Gazette for present month – price 1s. 6d postage 2d.> A Goulard & Son. 30 Henrietta St. Covent Garden

Sep. 13th. 1875. 10.30. A.M.
Corfe Castle
Breakfast Picnic. Tom. Katie. Mary. Emma. Hardy.[21]
Drove in Sommer's Van, leaving Swanage at 7. with 15 people picked up people on the road, until we were 21. & were packed as close as sardines. Fearful hills. Sommer making wicked witty remarks about them. "Lord – would save a lot of sins in him alone if he levelled the roads, it would be much better than building the Church" – etc. Horse out of condition. Another horse & man put on for part

of the way postilion style. A sweet-smelling clear morning   Sun shining carelessly & lazily. Brighter & hotter now – nearing Corfe – the scenery hilly & valleyey & rejoicing the eye. The castle high on the highest hill, tall masses of solid masonry – arches & blocks & walls stretching round a great distance – The village or town lying below, composed of very poor cottages – not pretty – but the church interesting. Aplin boiled our kettle & we brought up the tea-pot with tea made in it – a kettle of boiling water (& four cups – in a basket). We sat in a corner at the right where there is a low stone seat & looked down upon Corfe. About half past one Mary & Katie took their way to Wareham along a hot road, & we parted on King Edward's bridge, watched them out of sight   (First we scrambled all down the slope on that side of the castle.)

Drove home on top of the bus. Which was like being on a coach – Three horses abreast Plenty of jokes on the road from "Willshire" the man. A splendid day – fine breeze, fine hills, fine trees   A most beautiful road. Hedges flowing over into the wide-sided roads, growing freely into the fields behind. We sometimes passed into shaded parts the trees growing close to the road. Nuts trees reaching a good way up to them, the yellow ox eyes almost half way up to the nut trees – Near Corfe, is a Manor House – Mem – to see it.

Abroad get sugar stand & sugar slicer. Buy
curtain tassels & cords, or equivalents.

Ivy leaf from Balzac's grave [*leaf adhering to page with pencilled line around*]

Père-Lachaise   Paris

Diary 2

May–November 1876

Describing principally the visit to Holland,
the Rhine and the Black Forest (May–June 1876)

Diary of a Journey to
Holland; the Rhine,
Black Forest, &c.[22]
by E.L. Hardy.
1876.

[SKETCH]   First views of Holland like this

Nearing Holland at 9.AM a flat land on a level with the sea, trees little straight ones close to the edge of the water – many windmills – <u>very strange sight</u>

May 29. 1876.
Liverpool Station London: leaving by the 7. p.m. train for Harwich to cross to Rotterdam.[23]

In the train. 4 young women in couples at either end. Two, talking German – Beautiful sunset, prolonged afterglow –

All German ladies except one in the cabin – many babies   Smooth passage – sick when I was dressing in my berth which had bedclothes   The lady who was most important was very stout <u>& had a 5 week's old baby</u> –[24]

Drove to Scheveningen – a fishing village near the Hague – Stood on a sand hill or dyke – saw a red-roofed village beneath us at our right, & the sea & Dutch shipping at our left. This was a very characteristic view of Holland; grass growing thinly in the deep loose sand: stones laid down in it for a road part way – fine Hotels in the village. The sea the other side very much higher – broad fishing boat with no prow – sterns – [SKETCH] The people in this village have their wooden shoes painted white. After a jargon with our young driver, in which we try to explain that we want a drive through the town & then to the the station he takes us down an avenue & we lose sight of town to a park where we stopped with other carriages to listen to a nice band at a building. In the park lamps were swung occasionally from the trees across the park –

At the Hague. Just returned from seeing a train passing a road way   People waiting – man holding a white flag – little children near.

[*At top of the above page:* SKETCH]   Picture at the Hague   Paul Potter

The first class room at the Stations in Holland are restaurants   Policemen dressed like ours: so are the ladies, in last fashion   Working women's hats are huge things – House all have do[ub]le doors for their front entrance   ★ A high ornamental window on the roof in the centre like this: [SKETCH] Windows & doors all jammed together. Large windows. Women in Holland wear white caps of spotless whiteness & gold wires sticking out near their eyes from the sides of their faces [SKETCH]   sometimes a huge hat over it all but young women do not wear wires now. A cap, & English hat sometimes over it & a basket

June 2nd. 1876.[25] Travelling to Cologne from Rotterdam. After passing Utrecht the country becomes more agricultural & wooded. Young married people in train –

We had hot water at Rotterdam brought up in the morning in pint cups – two – Shrubs & trees in gardens like ours – laburnums in flower. All the people talk English.

Houses are peculiar in these respects – a great deal of glass but the windows rather plentiful than extending across the fronts as shop windows in England – yet large & long frame works always white & everything painted white that can be in the house & outside

Houses are narrow & high & all shaken together & apparently falling forward into the street – when they are first built they build the lower part forward so as to have a good foundation – then when they begin to shake forward out of the perpendicular they rivet them like old china thus – side of a house [SKETCH]   sometimes they build up a new front – but painting & repairing is always going on – Grass which grows upon the dyke at Scheveningen
[SKETCH]   Rivets in sides of Houses at Rotterdam

The flasket, basket or any burden on the head has always a pad, often this is very much ornamented

Tuesday 30 May 1876
Rotterdam – Breakfast at Bath Hotel

Cold meat, & yellow jelly – sugar in low glass dish – 3 sorts of rolls   Room with double glass doors at one end & a jib, door the other end, nice waiters, charming garden with English plants. Laburnums in flower. Large silver solid globe on a stand for ornament – a glaring shining thing – cats & kittens   A pleasant Hotel. Master of it showed us all over it.

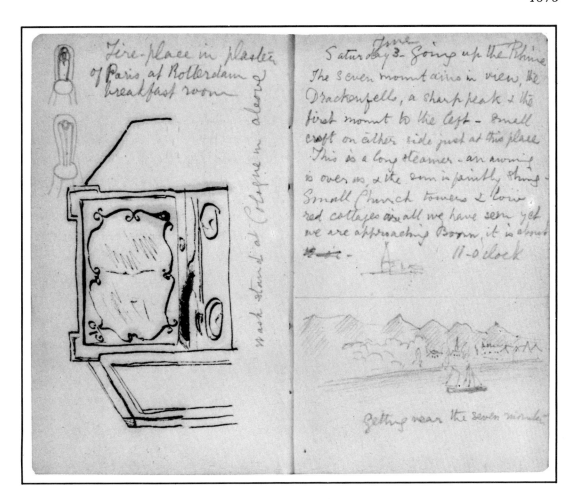

[SKETCH]   Fire-place in plaster of Paris, at Rotterdam breakfast room

[SKETCH]   Wash stand at Cologne in alcove

Saturday June 3 – Going up the Rhine
The seven mountains in view, the Drachenfels, a sharp peak & the first mount to the left – small croft on either side just at this place This is a long steamer: an awning is over us, & the sun is faintly shining. Small Church towers & low red cottages are all we have seen yet we are approaching Bonn, it is about 11 o'clock   [SKETCH]

[SKETCH]   Getting near the seven mountains

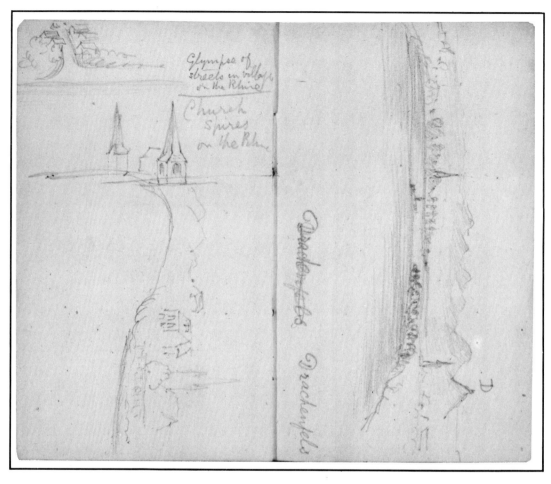

[SKETCH]   Glimpse of streets in village on the
Rhine
[SKETCH]   Church spires on the Rhine
[SKETCH]   Drachenfels

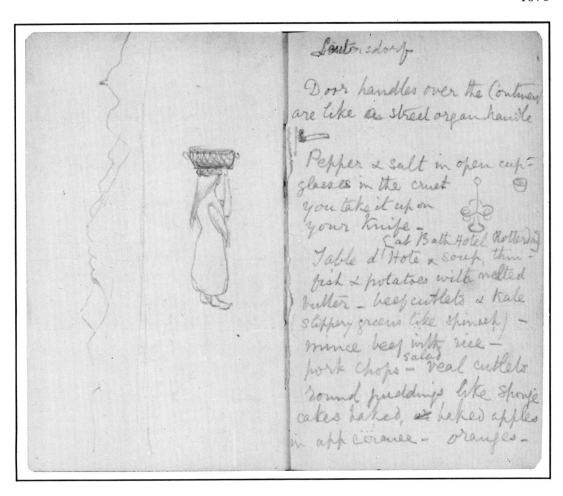

Lautersdorf

Door handles over the Continent are like a street organ handle. [SKETCH] Pepper & salt in open cup-glasses in the cruet [SKETCH] you take it up on your knife – (at Bath Hotel Rotterdam)

Table d'Hôte & soup, thin – fish & potatoes with melted butter – beef cutlets & kale (slippery greens like spinach) – mince beef with rice – pork chops – salad   veal cutlets round puddings like sponge cakes baked, baked apples in appearance – oranges

Cologne[26] – A bridge of boats to Deutz: which has a floating bridge – ie. a portion in the middle – two or three of the boats with platforms slowly moves aside, pulled by ropes, a steamer passes, the bridge is pulled back & the crowd waiting pass over in haste about their business – There is a railway bridge & at intervals there are towers on this one opposite each other – on other side – [SKETCH]

Tower of Dom –
Standing amidst flying-buttresses – gurgoyles

above us & figures of Faust & Mephistopheles the guide says with a smile of delight

Up at the top – a circular place & magnificent view all round of the winding Rhine & suburbs of Cologne Darmstadt & other places in the distance – below us a great bronze cross – roofs of houses cut slates in half circles   A forest of stonework beneath us of crocketted pinnacles –   [SKETCH]

Hôtel de Hollande Cologne
T. angry about the brandy flask   Narrow bedroom – bought Rhine-book

Market at Cologne on a Friday – women all wear white handkerchiefs over their heads. [SKETCH] Some wear nothing – no caps worn here – bought 2 oranges.

Went up the Rhine on Saturday – stopped at Coblenz opposite the fortress of Ehrenbreit-stein.

Saturday evening 4 June   Sitting up on the Asterstein an eminence near the Fortress

This afternoon just now we went up steep roads & steps to the Fortress of Ehrenbreit-stein – The sun shone blazingly upon a view the most magnificent I had ever seen – the town of Coblenz lay far at our feet, the size at that distance could be covered by a hat the rivers Rhine & Moselle meeting at a direct angle & Coblenz filling the angle   The view the other side very beautiful, & we looked down upon towers & square-standings & a road on which the soldiers were mere dots – moving – Hôtel de Geant – Coblenz

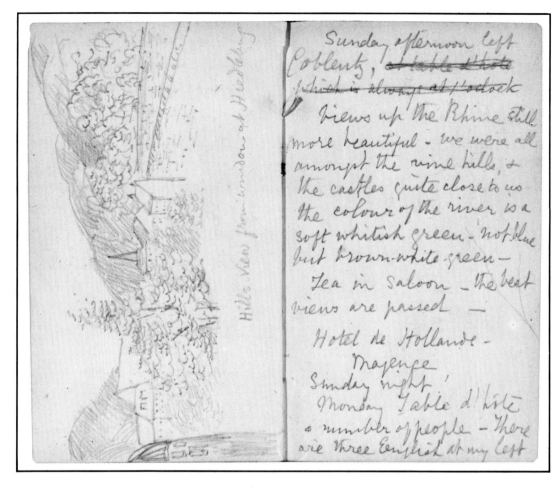

[SKETCH]   Hills   View from window at Heidelberg

Sunday afternoon left Coblenz, <at table d'hôte which is always at 1 o'clock>

Views up the Rhine still more beautiful – we were all amongst the vine hills, & the castles quite close to us   the colour of the river is a soft whitish green – not blue but brown-white-green –

Tea in saloon – the best views are passed –

Hôtel de Hollande – Mayence, Sunday night

Monday   Table d'hôte a number of people – There are three English at my left.

We are at the end of a long table & a fat English lady sits at the top who keeps fanning herself   A splendid band playing in the room opposite. A very high class, rich hotel –

A confirmation in cathedral in the morning, two girls in white at the dinner table[27] – Highly decorated Hôtel Cathedral at Mainz, & a Church with an altar. Very elaborate

[SKETCH]   Altar with Candles

Mirrors between windows   Pillow cases of finest lawn edges with patent frilling. Two beds, cots

Heidelberg – Tuesday June 9. Going up to Castle which is a magnificent one   Still solid stonework. One part a museum. Saw Mary Q. of Scots head, after she had been on the block in a picture there – Great tun like a hull of ship. A gallery like a howdah on top. Court jester standing near – Very hot – Restoration in Castle grounds. Afterwards went to the great terrace & had a beautiful view – Plants are very beautiful – everywhere we go, shrubs in flower   Spirea, double, Syringa & a catkin kind of shrub   The feathery tufts lying on the ground. Climbed up to the tower by rugged steps & slippery places, wished I had not. Intensely hot, immensely tired, a mist spread everywhere   Saw nothing[28] – great fatigue next day –

Double staircases with mirrors at Heidelberg.

Parsley over fried potatoes   Eggs brought on the table at breakfast at Mainz in hot water in basin with spoon –

Table d'Hôte

Potato soup, fried slices of fish (with meat gravy, or) melted butter in a boat – boiled beef very coarse in small slices   potatoes – then a course of asparagus, spinach with melted butter in a boat – mutton chops & ham sausages – then a queer dish – of eggs beaten up, covering fish-cakes   parsley put over it, cooked – – fowl & little plates by the left side for fruit, preserved plum, cherries, etc handed round to eat with fowl slices – Dish of puddings or ice creams with biscuits

Hôtel Holland
Baden-Baden
One large room like a ball room   White &
gold ornamentations festooned mirrors &
Grecian pillars & scarlet furniture in velvet
Mauerwein – in flask-bottle at Baden   Oxen
driven at Heidelberg & at Baden   Window
blinds, only let down at night, as there are
short curtains to window panes, these blinds
are fringed, scolloped iron run in, at 3 or 4
inches from the bottom – made of fine damask
for the purpose –

[SKETCH]   Stove at Karlsruhe[29]   All much
alike – sometimes shorter – sometimes
bronze   sometimes marble – sometimes –
oftenest of porcelain glazed

Mem – Drove from the Hotel at Baden to the Black Forest in an open carriage (fresh weather, lovely, before the thunderstorm) through the gardens – black hills opposite

At the Castle – a small magnificent one – we went out on the balcony   beautiful view. Sitting on chairs (& little tables) looking down on the river & mountains of the Black Forest – Hills & hills a perfect scene   A turmoil of mountains   Small rafts floating down. Managed with difficulty for the stream is shallow & encumbered with shoals of sand – a difficult stream – men like ants, so far below us – Went into vineyard, vines half grown up their sticks – grapes just formed – Trees firs tipped with green   Vines, trees, shrubs grass all a tender green – 12.30 P.M. (Like Bickleigh Vale, Dartmoor etc. on a gigantic scale –

Thursday – In the train – Going to Baden – First view of the Black Forest – the peaked hills, not far distant   Faint blue ones behind – Baden-Baden a more beautiful and extensive Heidelberg – houses & gardens public & private, trees shrubs houses hills banks of green all mixed up – Beautiful drive through the Black Forest   Thunderstorm afterwards – Began to feel very ill – The gardens & fountain at Baden beautiful – Saw the famous gaming rooms – heard concert at night –

Strasbourg – Felt very ill. Had brandy – Saturday morning – Saw the Cathedral – & the Clock at the hour of noon – A thick crowd – Cock crew 3 times. Very weak & ill. Ulcerated throat – feel as if I was either recovering from or going to have a fever[30] – Long roofs & many windows in them   Tall chimneys & storks on top

[SKETCH]   View of spire from our window at Strasbourg

Slates of roof cut round everywhere
Hotel like <u>cloisters</u> at Strasbourg   a square
not street <u>in front</u>   Left Strasbourg Saturday   Came to Metz at night. 11. Left Metz
wet Sunday   Came to Brussels by slow train
– from half past 12 to. 9. Hôtel de la Poste,
"Fosse aux Loups". Brussels. Old part of the
Town. Monday went to field of Waterloo. By
train to station then by train, then walked a
mile   bought photographs of a guide –
stopped at Hôtel de Musée opposite the Lion
Mount –
    Mem. Monday June 12. 1876.
It was a <u>lovely</u> day – & plenty of air, even
breezes but hot sunshine – many flowers – a
broad expanse of corn fields – rye – no <u>heights</u>
to be seen – went up the steps & saw <u>all</u> over
the field, & read the account, guides were
disturbing with their talk then lunched at
Hotel – saw Museum – skulls, weapons, hair.
Niece of Edward Cotton shows the Museum
– Walked to – Hougoumont. (Much crimson
clover in the field)   Hougoumont small
ruins, low walls to the orchard, buttresses
fallen away – Glass of water inside, whilst
drinking it, went into the kitchens & saw
scraps of weapons   Old chapel with crucifix
& altar with wooden virgin

Tuesday seeing Brussels

Very small, one window up high, looked like
a little out-house, & a common door just like
it – ruins   Two or three small window
frames   Iron bars, & the remains of a garden
wall with balustrades which were much hid-
den, & lay in the grass mostly, dividing the
orchard – where were two graves   Bridg-
man – and latter old Cotton himself – (B fell
there) Then walked to La Belle Alliance
Young woman with infant, sold us a glass of
delicious milk each (black stove, huge wardrobe) – Then walked to La Haye Sainte – The
largest & best farm house   very large courtyard, very large house inside – young woman
ironing in spacious stone room at left –
cupboard or a small cellarette opposite front
door, as at Kirland,[31]   This door had bullet
marks – then went down passage to right –
one kitchen at right. Small iron barred window – room to left   a small room with small
barred window. At the right of this window,
in an alcove, or extension was the well; we
looked down   deep & black – & many men
could be thrown into it; the room & well both
in use – room back or dirty kitchen to the
house, sloppy and crowded with pots & pans,
scarcely room – Turned then to the front
room to the right of front door – bread & cake
just baked   Under a basket of bread

woman brought out a basket of skulls – teeth perfect   Then gave us some light cake & little child ran into garden & gave me flowers – guelder roses & peony – walked back through Mont St Jean & Waterloo – saw house where Victor Hugo wrote the last of Les Misérables called Hôtel de Colonnes – These villages very long & roughly paved – Mont St. J. very quiet. Waterloo, larger house   Round cupola   Church – closed. Long walk to station – great fatigue, so ended Waterloo day.[32] Today I am still greatly fatigued, & Tom is cross about it – Just been to see lace made in one of the manufactories or "Fabriques de dentelle" – Had a drive round the city – Bought cravat-ends for 4/2d ie – 5 francs –

Mem – From the Lion's Mount the field of Waterloo is spread out from Wellington's position, & Hougoumont & the rest seem near: the two armies were so close together – When we got past La Belle Alliance & between it & La Haye Sainte the ground seemed to rise a little at our left –

Hay-making going on round us, & we walked in a narrow path through the high grain; wooden shoes, a drinking can & the voices of the field workers – Villagers very few & quiet in Mt St Jean – more in Waterloo

Carrying a white petticoat from the wash on a hand-peg or frame   Dog-carts in Brussels –

Mem – Strasbourg – the altar in Cathl. mean-looking, west end altar, the other scaffolding alterations, a flight of steps to altar, archway underneath   Service going on –

Mem – at Cologne – a corpse lying in state – friends taking away the candle-stick, service just over –

[SKETCH]
Long green glasses for dear wine, at table d'Hôte, Mayence & Heidelberg

Beautiful public gardens at Coblenz, every variety of surprise, in the way of pavilion, ornamental seats, archways, festoons
[SKETCH]   creepers trained up wires, & straight wires supporting, – Green crimson blue globes on sticks, & up in shrubs as ornaments – lovely views of the river in outer walks, all walks leading into each other –

Mem – at Mainz dinner Swiss cottage Wire frames with biscuits all down the table – Music man with music in hand, came round for money – Dinner – *fish-soup* slices of beef & radishes – beans, with milk over them & slices of dried salmon – then a mess of eggs & meat, omelette I suppose Then joints of fowl with salad & cherries –

Blackman's [SKETCH] Cotton's [SKETCH]
The stone graves in the orchard at Hougoumont –
A man building a wall had just found a bullet in a brick – at Hougoumont[33]
Thunder storm at Bruxelles –

Dinner at Hôtel le Poste Bruxelles   Vermicelli soup   Brains   Turbot with butter & capers   Beef & spinach   Pigeons & tomato sauce   Broccoli & butter sauce   Mutton   Poultry   Tartelettes with fresh strawberries & preserved syrup over them   Oranges & biscuits –

Aerated water bottle, basket-wine-bottle on the Table – Thunder & rain, walked through kitchens – servants dining at 1 – Mem. Tartelettes with fraises   "Tartelettes aux fraises"

Brussels Wednesday morning
About one o'clock – Tom is gone to see the picture gallery which was closed yesterday so I have missed it altogether   Quite worn out with the day at Waterloo – walked yesterday from the picture gallery to a lace manufactory & back to hotel   Election going on yesterday – Just now we have returned from seeing the cathedral – a wedding going on in side chapel. Candles in wire stands like flower stands at the altar to the Virgin (a beautiful figure in blue & white with a sweet face) at our left. The bride in white is set off by the yellow satin dress of the priest who turns his face to the high altar & his back to her – he is spangling with jewels – a service going on in the nave, not finished – we had waited so long for the wedding to begin that we became tired before it was over & left :–

Figures of saints very fine down west end of nave between the capitals of columns –

A large building in Brussels in one of the squares has a very richly painted & gilded pediment –

Mem – at Strasbourg & Metz had little silver baskets hung on to spout of teapot –

Mem – young lady with alpen-stock got out at Saarbruck.

A great many of the shops in Brussels are like fine private homes – no open door or shop front – The name & goods are printed large outside only – [SKETCH] Lace workers Across a court was a room with open French windows – near the windows were sitting the worker with the lace cushions on their laps – dull heavy ugly weary looking women. Made me sad – one only was young & almost pretty, so cheerful   Probably going to be married, she had a cornelian ring on a finger

Tables were put down the room made with cushions and rounded tops – These are for shawls, fichus & large articles on which two or more women work –

Their fingers play, as on a piano-reel – or bobbin – [SKETCH]   It has a handle which their fingers lightly pass about & make heaps of them from side to side –   [SKETCH] cushion

Leaving Brussels – Just before Table d'Hôte dinner   Ladies passing through the courtyard to it – an aviary –

Station at Brussels, rather handsomer, room d'attente has two rows of columns. Between each are seats 3 sides of a square in green velvet   A book stall in centre –

Saw the Duchess of Richmond's house – at corner of street like the others   long white french windows – to distinguish it, the upper portion of windows are painted pink –[34]

Mem   The cathedral bell at Metz the deepest tone I ever heard

Wednesday afternoon came to Antwerp – Everything in draper's shops "Nouveauté anglaise, also in print shops little things – had some wine at a cafe – processions passing by, election time, a riot the day before. Saw a house a café where the windows had been smashed – Cathedral spire elegant like lace Even clock is a mere frame work. Houses squeezed against it – Thursday went inside service going on, people kneeling about everywhere – candles lit & dying out in side chapels – beautiful chapels, with shrines & pictures behind the high altar

Saw Reuben's "Descent from the cross', & Elevation of the cross & Assumption of the virgin – at the right hand just as you enter –

Sitting in the centre   At our left behind a white railing is a service at a carved altar with lighted candles – a bell ringing like an atmosphere bell – everybody turns their chair at the second ringing – even the old snuffy women who are clearing off the chairs – 3 or 4 times the bell rings, & heads are bowed – A wonderful carved pulpit with peacocks & birds

The pictures by Rubens are covered at 12. o'clock

A large carved cross hangs from the roof at chancel – In centre of nave is a carved figure of Christ standing – with pots of flowers all round the stand & high brass or gilt candle sticks – A mass of gilded things all down one aisle & people praying towards the shrines – A great many confessionals, each having angels or saints carved as large as life – The Cathedral itself is a plain one & has no capitals to its pillars   A white fan-roof– but the pictures & shrines enrich it.

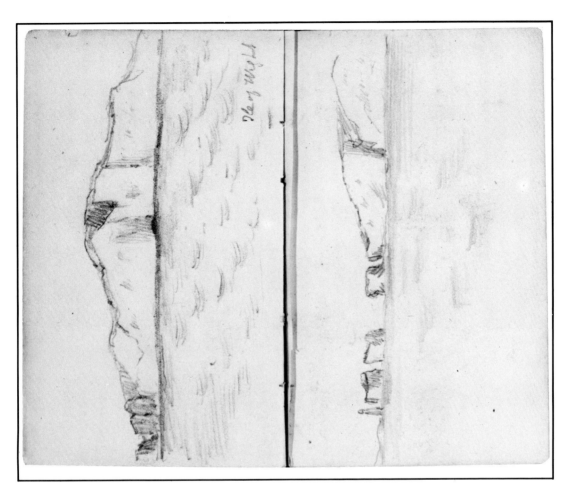

[SKETCH] Isle of Wight

[SKETCH]

[SKETCH]   Steamer. "Heather Bell." Going
from Swanage to Ryde & all

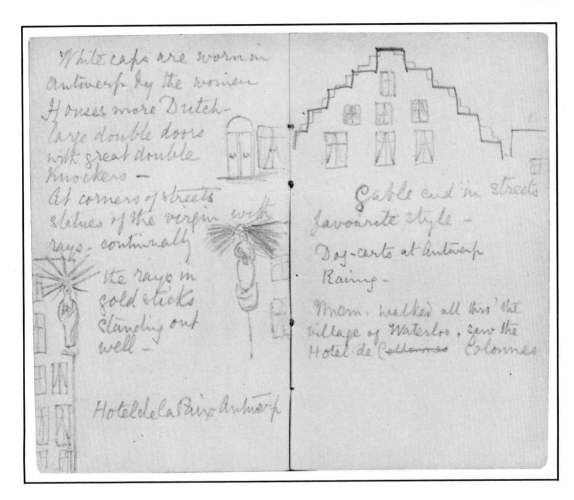

White caps are worn in Antwerp by the women   Houses more Dutch – large double doors with great double knockers – [SKETCH] At corners of streets statues of the virgin with rays continually the rays in gold sticks standing out well –   [SKETCH]

[SKETCH]   Hôtel de la Paix. Antwerp

[SKETCH]   Gable end in streets favourite style –

Dog-carts at Antwerp   Raining –

Mem. Walked all thro' the village of Waterloo, saw the Hôtel de Colonnes

Picture Gallery at Antwerp –

In Vestibule, portraits of Rubens & other masters with pupils

Exquisite pictures & very large, some of them have been in Cathedrals.

The crucifixion, a triptych – Agonized thief has torn his foot from the nail – The figure of centurion as he sits on his horse is wonderfully good, & Mary at right is most perfect in effect – a wonderful picture –

Pool Bethseda – Man taking up a mattress, a lot of it in foreground & a small stream trickling amidst stones –

Adoration of Magi –

Mary is rather fleshy & earthly beautiful & smiles much – The eyes of the Magi are directed upon her in a most striking style – the chief figure like an Arab has great eyes glaring at her – the others look sceptical – Mem – eyes

Quentin Massys

Metallic in style generally especially the robe of the

daughter of Herodias in the wing of The dead Christ"   Christ's limbs much distorted & the handling of the body is very tender & loving by the women

Doubting Thomas –

The hand with red hole very natural, so are apostles' faces –

Christ in God the Father's arms   Horrible picture

Martyrdom of saints, Hideous

St Anna teaching Virgin

A great number of sacred subjects, heads of virgins & repentant pictures –

Chimes (Carillon) at Antwerp – like a musical-box

Table d'hôte – excited politicians   3 men opposite quite a study   [SKETCH]

Leave Antwerp today

Friday at 4. P.M

Mt. Calvary in St. Peter's Church – a garden at the side – made of grotto work figures of saints & apostles about 60 standg in various position, old tower steps ornament the pathway, high up facing you is a wall of rock work & apostles, Christ on the Cross at the top – at one side

He is a little child's

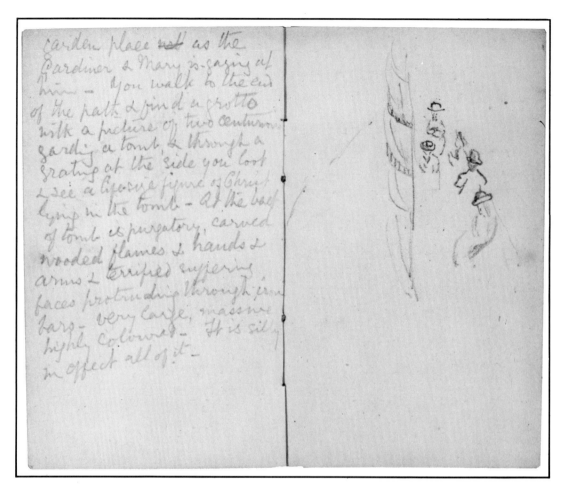

garden place as the Gardener & Mary is gazing at him – You walk to the end of the path & find a grotto with a picture of two centurions gazing on tomb, & through a grating at the side you look & see a life-size figure of Christ lying in the tomb – At the back of tomb is

purgatory, carved wooded flames & hands & arms & terrified suffering protruding through iron bars – very large, massive highly coloured – It is silly in effect all of it –

[SKETCH]

Going back to England where we have no home & no chosen county[35]

18. June. 1876 –

Sunday – Came yesterday morning to Norfolk Hotel   Went this morning to Chelsea Hospital.[36] Had a chat with <u>Bentley</u>[37] after the service –

Luggage searched at
Rotterdam
Emmerick
Sterpnich [*sic*]
Harwich[38]

July 3. 1876
Riverside Villa   Sturminster Newton[39]
Oct. 26. (Thursday –) Dined at Loundes'
Oct. 31. (Tuesday) Willie & Walter came
Nov. 2. They left at 8. AM.
(Mrs. D. called Tues Oct 31. –)
Nov 13 Notice to Geo –
Nov 14. Luncheon at Mrs. Dashwood's,[40]
met Mr. Mrs. Miss. Warrey –[41]

[SKETCH]   raft on Rhine

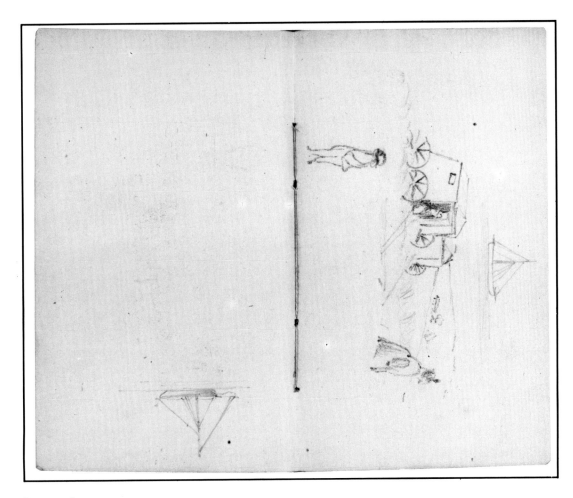

[SKETCH]

[*Caption to sketch on previous page:*]
View from our window at the Hôtel de
Hollande   Cologne – First View of the
Rhine. 7.P.M.

[SKETCH]

Diary 3

March–April 1887

The Visit to Italy

Italy

1887: Monday 14th March.[42] Fine day. East wind, left Max Gate Dorchester for London by 10.20. Tuesday morning left Holborn station for Calais. Cold, but snow storm of previous day had dried up. On leaving London, snow came on thick, & we had heavy snow nearly all the way catching only glimpses of the hop & orchard country through which I had never passed before. All umbrellas opened on leaving the carriages to walk along the wharf to the vessel, which we entered in the worst possible plight, thick fog & driving snow, the fog horn blown every second.[43] It seemed the height of madness to start.   Tom went below, I stayed on deck, scarcely any movement perceptible. I thought the novelty of a calm passage & the short route was delightful, it was increased unpleasantly by the more delightful sensation of apprehension

Before we had gone far – the fog horn
suddenly ceased. Presently the men passed me
in procession with hard brooms & began
brushing up the snow & casting it overboard.
I watched it going on. Then sat up feeling the
brightness of affairs the sun shone down. I
tried walking about, then looked out a length
of time through the port-hole, enjoying the
sight of the sea. I only observed one or two
vessels in the distance, not the traffic going on
like vehicles in London streets as Tom had
described it during the fog & snow storm.
Our fellow-passenger, the amateur photogra-
pher, was lying down nearby all the time. He
& we were together again in the train going to
Paris. Also a handsome coquettish French
lady in a wonderful new shaped bonnet which
became her well. & her husband, an attentive,
chatty man.

She sat bolt upright the whole time so as not to disarrange herself. & smiled & chatted back to him indefatigably. The train stopped at Amiens, we drank a few mouthfuls of coffee, it was between 5 & 6 o'c, then we rushed back, I could not easily find the carriage, our friend did not appear, his luggage only was with us. Next day, train stopped at Dijon. We went to the buffet & found a dinner ready, excellent dinner soup, fish patty   Beef and potato mashed   Fowl spinach   Vanilla cream etc. Paid 6 francs each   Tom very vexed. Dyspeptic before and worse now. Afterwards the train stopped somewhere while we were talking, we forgot to ask if we should change   The train moved on in an opposite direction & caused us great worry. On enquiry next station found we were at Culoz, & all right for Aix. Arrived there found we had come through heavy snow. It was lying deep around us, found

a carriage with a deep overhanging hood to it, awaiting us, & slowly drove up hill through biting wind & heavy snow to this hotel Château Durieux on the hills at past 12 o'clock.[44] Very cheerful place comfortable room. Bright fire on hearth had a tray with milk and hot water eau de vie & biscuits brought up – warmed ourselves thoroughly & slept well. Stayed in bed till past ten next morning. Deep snow next day Thursday[45]
Sat in cosy little room by fire after breakfast[46]   The hotel undergoing painting & refurnishing for the season. It cleared up, saw the mountain from window –[47] walked out to the Baths L'Etablissements   Woman speaking English showed us – very spacious building   Very numerous & varied rooms for bathing different parts of the body – knees particularly   Went up hill at back of it, banks of snow in streets, women washing at hot spring

Sun came out, mists cleared a little   Had glimpses of mountains. Dinner served in same little room, tall Savoyard woman waiting. She kept plates on the stove (long narrow baskets of wood for fire). We waited, because another cover was laid, wondering who would appear – ugly man – something in general appearance nose etc. like Tillard. A Yorkshire man going to stay some weeks sketching. Sorry to lose, asked if T.H. was the author. I wrote our names in the visitor's book.

Left at 6 am next morning, rose at 5 o'c. Had coffee & milk, drove in hooded carriage to station. Snow still lying about early morning most beautiful. Saw the mountain with a pink glow on them, very lovely. The Salle d'Attente very comfortable – heated with a grating to put your feet on. Got into a carriage which was occupied by a young couple on their wedding tour. They had had a night journey & we had awoke them. The air was very close   The snow had drifted through the window ledges & the frost had been severe. We opened the shutters, & after a while a window & aired it. The other couple, settled themselves in a sitting position & still napped on their pillows, she had a veil tied round her head like a hood & they both looked aged & odd. After an hour of dozing on their part & excitement fidgetting & admiration on ours. They finally aroused themselves, & we chatted in French to him, she could not speak a word. He told us they had spent 8 days in Paris, had had a guide. Read out from his note book the places they had seen. More than we had – On the way past Modane, the conductor found our tickets had not been used at Modane he got into the carriage with us to talk about our Italian fellow traveller, told him we were English, we explained as well we could that no one had asked for our tickets   He told me to be at ease about it, he would get them done if we wrote our names on them. Tom began and we rushed into a tunnel, When we came out he wrote half a stroke and we went into another – It was a long time before we could write our names – which we did so distinctly that the conductor was in great admiration.

He jumped out at a little station and carried off the whole lot. To our great consternation We recriminated & grew more and more uneasy about them. Thought we should have to stay at Turin till they were sent on or perhaps never see any more & have to pay twice over. At the next place, he suddenly appeared & the relief was ecstatic. Took a cab &

drove a long way through the town to the Hôtel Trombetta Via Roma. Very fine hotel – beautifully decorated Salon à manger   Went out, had Italian at a café   Horrid stuff. Went down through the arcaded streets to the River Po   The bridge, very beautiful view from it, an eminence beyond & a round church in a square – heavy snow overtook us – got into a train as far as we could, stood under shelter at the Palace Madama. When it cleared got back to our hotel. Dined, very few people. Two ladies came later, one by ourself opposite gazing all the time at me. Next morning went out, down the same & being fine weather we climbed up the eminence to a monastery & Alpine Club house a wooded height a magnificent view of the town. A sunny morning but too misty to see the distant mountains. A more beautiful eminence to our right, no time to go there, a train conveys people up to it. La Superga, a palace. Left at about 2 o'clock, I alarmed just before starting because Tom had taken another little stroll by himself, & the time was up & omnibus waiting & I looking up & down the English – shopped & people clothed streets. Colouring of houses very yellow   French windows & shutters and red roofs –

Two gentlemen in train – Italian gentlemen wear black gloves. When we came to Genoa[48] caught peeps of the Mediterranean & shipping dull weather, no blue sea. A row of omnibuses   One Hôtel Smith quite full, turned out to be Germans & Americans   All laughed because other omnibuses all empty which belonged to the grandes hôtels – drove a jolting journey through the streets to the hotel on the quay. Mr S. a little man, very English – hotel quaint. Very spotless, view, the harbour.

Tent bed, iron with muslin curtains. After dinner went out about 8 o'clock along the quay a little way & returned as it seemed too dark & dismal & adventuresome. Opened the window & gazed out   got sore throats Went to bed early, noise on wharves. Next morning found an American in drawing room who had been through the earthquakes at San Remo, & described his feelings – the hotel he was in being at the corner of the street & he having a corner room, but the house was built by the engineers of the Mt. Cenis tunnel & was built of solid blocks   It would take a good earthquake to shake it down. Went out to see the town, visited took a cab (1½ francs, he asked 2 francs) drove to Palazzo Doria, Méry's palace described in Les Nuits Italiennes)   Very ancient, two or three beautiful rooms, shown by a porter (bitterly cold wind always here) paintings &

statuary of the Doria family. Cardinal & Pope one chamber had been <was> a bedroom, no bed but a smaller & less rich chamber. I sat in a chair just as Méry says he did, in the salon the ceiling was painted richly.

We then went to two others, entering one timidly, no porter appeared, courts of dazzling marble with columns of same, & steps to other halls with corinthian columns as before, then seeing glass doors open we entered   I first, with trepidation, walked up splendid flights of whitest marble steps, very clean, marble walls, like the song "I dreamt", Then a lady appeared   I enquired in French if it was open to the public & she said yes to view the pictures. We found doors & a bell. I rang, a servant appeared, & opened readily to us. Showing us the way in, & through magnificent rooms furnished with gilded & marbled furniture

with pictures by the best Italian painters
Frescoes, ceilings, inlaid marble floors. Gobelin tapestry, vases. Sèvres & Dresden glass
cases of them, pictures innumerable glowing
rich, Van Dycks & others, showed us the
grand salons, then allowed us to peep into the
rooms used by occupiers, smaller drawing
rooms, very richly furnished, wonderful
chandeliers everywhere wrapped up in taffeta
muslin, (like ice) to be bought at Soleils in
Genoa somewhere. The two last rooms in one
palace had Maple furniture & were simply
luxurious in English style, so we did not look
at them   Went to the next just opposite,
found an orangery & fine rooms with still
more splendid pictures, one St Jerome very
fine. Also a picture modern, done in mosaic,
of a tiger with a dark back –

ground, a marvellous piece of work, took 8 years to do, the guide servant was him self delighted with it. Tom gave these men a franc. Peeped into many churches lots of worshippers, bells going all day. Some shops open, many worshippers coming out of the churches. The lower class of women most gorgeous in dress, no particular style, except that handkerchiefs were worn over the head & tied behind the neck often of a bright colour, sometimes black – a group continually passing of three or four women in harmonious colours, chiefly of blue, bright blue & darker, purple orange kerchief, green gown darker red shawl – much red, & much more blue to be seen. Bright colours everywhere, house yellow, salmon colour very often, sometimes pink. A jammed sensation, on account of the narrowness of streets & great height of houses, palaces continually views of narrow streets, going up hill or downhill, looking like gullies, figures passing in brilliant colours. Which if seen <by> sunlight must be beautiful   We came back & rested awhile & took our quinine, I put on a warmer jacket, & we took another drive keeping our carriage close this time before we had it open & it was wretched cold, We drove up hill, catching peeps of the sea between the high houses & winding slowly up to the crest of the hill where we got out & a sight burst upon our view which I shall never forget – the whole city lay before us, & the sea – the Mediterranean beyond the houses seemed compressed in a solid mass as if without squares or streets, at the left, a mass of colour. Red

& blue & green & purple, the rest, a soft harmonious mosaic rich as the colouring in the church of St Ouen at Rouen   Blue hills beyond at our back shutting in this city of marble palaces & houses   I never saw such a superb city, Oh if there had been sunlight poured upon it, what a sight it would have been. However it was fine & dry, & there was one golden cloud stretching out to the west, & the sea was rather blue.

Walked down to the wharf & then I came back & T.H. went out again. I found the same black cat prowling about & whilst calling, the Japanese child came with the chambermaid, & we all went to look at the picaninis, & they were in a little loft-like chamber, but on the same floor, on straw, 4 little tabbies, the child & I made friends over them   She was a [illegible] a Japanese, who it seems had picked her up by chance, a little waif, & become her benefactor – an intelligent child, she gave me a kiss, & I saw her afterwards   She came to dinner after we had finished. I wrote this in the drawing room –

At Genoa frequent groups of women in brilliant yet harmonious colouring – yellow or red. Kerchief on head, crimson gown, scarlet shawl darker red, or brighter on others dark blue, light blue, orange, purple, green, 4 or 5 women. – Not so frequent nor so brilliant at Florence but here at F. the waggon, long narrow one horse ones have always a scarlet horse cloth, either rolled up or thrown right over the animal, resting on the shafts & over its head, & folds & hanging down at the sides, most picturesque & graceful

Came to Florence on Monday, had an Italian gentleman in the train with a reading lamp. A linguist, talked in English to us, 'the train was "late". Mr. & Mrs. Baxter[49] had a carriage waiting for us & we drove here,[50] Mrs. MacNamee was gone to the Theatre Mr & Mrs. B. came upstairs to the bedroom & then left us, we had milk & hot water & unpacked. Next morning went out, nearly lost our way. Saw the square where Savonarola was burnt. & the bridge where Dante first see Beatrice (the etching we have at home) Got back had lunch, lots of people in this Pension Travellers going & coming. American many of them Mrs. B & her sister came to see us, went out to see the city & bought gloves. Saw the interior

of the Mausoleum of the Medici family &
church close by

Wednesday. Wet day   Drove to the Pitti
Palace[51] picture gallery, saw Raphael & other
great paintings. Had tea with the Baxters'
girls & Father & all, then came back to dinner.
Talked in the drawing-room & came into this
bedroom to write this. Tom is quite wearied
out & in his bed. Have some apprehensions
about Rome, people warn us about the fever,
but Mrs. B. assures us there is nothing to fear.

On our way from Genoa here, we stopped
an hour or so at Pisa.[52] Went up the tower,
very strange sensation. The ringers & a posse
of girls scampered up, the bells lifting &
swinging quite close to us, so that we could
not pass round the tower

Thursday went out in the morning as far as
the Cathedral, feeling very weary

The Duomo – Florence

Exquisite tone of bells chiming for service
<u>very</u> deep & melodious, could not attend to
anything else. Heard the bells of the city every
morning before rising & in the night. Went
into the Cathedral, heard or rather saw a
service going behind a glass screen. The
muslin garment of young boy or acolyte very
much, & very finely pleated & gathered like a
smock frock only more elaborate.

Afternoon went to Mrs Baxter's calling for
her to take us to her sisters in the country,
drove there in an open carriage   Beautiful
drive, through tall pinetrees called the Imper-
ial road in Italian. Looked over Florence.

Mrs. Dun's house very old & quaint   The
furniture 200 years old   The house 500. Saw
the old ploughs, oil jars, ox, cows, farm yard,
etc

Had tea, old mantel piece let into wall. All the children except the youngest <u>Lilly</u>, like the Florentines the eldest daughter speaks English with a very foreign aspect, & quite ungrammatically. Views of convent   Christopher Columbus house (with 2 wings to it) & mountains. Fine Italian countenance the farm man possessed.

Italian suavity. When we drove home this morning from the cathedral square the horse was weak, & I resolved to speak about to the man who, was delighted to have any interest taken in his horse & gratified at my patting it, which took me quite by surprise as I had expected an offensive reply as a cabman would have given for certain in London.

No grass will grown in the towns

in Italy, so the squares are all gravelled & rolled etc. One lady tried to get up a lawn & failed, after great expense.

At Pisa we passed a little church called Santa Maria de Pineta or Lady of the Thorn Remarkable for statuary of which it seemed composed, like an ivory toy placed there, a carved chessman or box the outline being statues standing up against the sky.

The echo in the Baptistery was a rolling sound as if an organ were playing though the guide only uttered two or three notes – most wonderful   He was pleased himself at the effect he produced & did it again.

Had some lunch at an Inn near the station at Pisa, very bad smell in that hotel, dragged our luggage across to the station. Came to Florence in about 3 hours I believe.

Italian politeness. On leaving train a passenger 2nd class from Florence to Rome took off his hat & said to us "Buon viaggio"

A dance given by Mrs. Macnamee to her friends & friends of visitors once a week Fridays – Last night March 25, we just looked in to the drawing room a few minutes to see the dancers, it had been converted into a ball room. Full dress, refreshments, piano, partners strolling in gallery, we in our room packing up. The dancing went on late.

Scenery from Genoa to Pisa along the shores of the Mediterranean, dull colours, leaden sky – rocks, sea, gardens villas, orange groves olive plantations sloe hedges, peach blossom – villas & cottages. Scarlet geraniums on walls along the ground anywhere like nasturtiums   Trains. Tunnels incessantly.

Scenery from Pisa to Florence   The Apennines close to us
Viaducts continually in Italy –

Scenery from Florence to Rome.
Mountains at distance, marshes near cultivated lands, fig trees pollard. Low like spread hand – rows of them along channels cut across fields, vines, hung upon them, figures on ladders training them sometimes, oxen & plough stony, land, but green corn growing between the fig & vine rows.

Went to Mrs Baxter's after dinner Friday for an hour or two, she had quite a party. Miss Marzials, Gosse's[53] friend Lilly youngest <u>Baxter</u> played violoncello, Lulu, second <u>Baxter</u> <u>played</u> in quartet, about 20 people there.

Stood in the morning under the shelter of the Loggia Lanzi, whilst a heavy shower of rain scattered the people, & the others laughed loudly – observed the exquisite statuary there   Then walked to the Croce church. It appeared to us at the end of a street. Dazzling white marble & at last against a blue Italian sky & sun shine for almost first time – Interior very beautiful, tomb of Michael Angelo Assisi frescoes.

White houses with flatter roofs

than ours, but not so flat as in the east all over the country, sometimes a soft buff colour – pretty towns all along the route. Writing this in train going to Rome.

Have seen sheep, oxen ploughing, & black pigs. Then droves of oxen ox carts, carrying hay etc. – goats grazing, horses, dogs on rails eating food thrown by passengers.

About 2.30 entering the Campagna   Fine mountains   Just past this is a plain with a range of hills behind the Tiber winds considerably, so that we keep passing & repassing it, over bridge & two viaducts.

Saturday March 26 came to Rome[54] Blue sky, cold wind. The environs ordinary Hedges & meadows like Dorchester & Fordington Field

Drove round Rome. Saw Forum (2) Trajan pillar. Colosseum   Giovanni Church. Sunday, walked out then drove through Rome to St. Peters. Walked down the Corso both days, had coffee at Caffee.

The large fashionable shops & people & carriages give it the appearance of an ordinary city. Disappointing – but the old streets, & gaily attired women of lower orders look right –

St. Peter's, very stately with solid piers having pilasters of coloured marble, scarcely any candles in the chapels, and scarcely any chapels, no pictures, no statues of the Virgin no tinsel ornaments whatever but little domes in aisles like the big dome, & the lights concentrated round the tomb of St. Peter

No tombstones on floor, hardly any seats, Cupola over the tomb first attracting the eye, large groups of statues occasionally Exterior very imposing, flights of steps scarcely marked were rising up a hill with colonnades of all round three sides, an enormous sweep of them and statues against the sky all round, deep-blue sky, large statues.

Great leathern doors, heavy to move.

St. Giovanni a perfect contrast   All gorgeous with the richest gilding, fresh frescoes, very fresh & beautiful pictures, making you realize why frescoes were adopted.

A blaze of gilding & coloured marbles & pictures.

Santa Maria Novella – a handsome church – but full of trash, innumerable altars, a dirty Italian man went – knelt down before a huge bouquet A little chapel above with steps up & a very trashy altar full of artificial flowers, two ladies praying before it.

Santa Croce, with fine statuary, & frescoes of Giotto, disappointing like the pictures of old masters, & Gobelin tapestry, so faded, these chapels narrow with high pointed arches
[SKETCH]

Little shoe-black persistent at Forum Sunday morning, broke my umbrella beating him off.

Beggars innumerable, hold back the leather doors

sometimes. Fine but cold Sunday
Shops open morning, shut evening, people in best clothes going to church, Queen & another lady in violet costumes complete drove by   crimson liveries, people bowing. We in café saw the King just before.

Clocks here in Rome have not the rich tone of those in Florence.

Cats with collars in the Forum
Long bread, pipe-like at Turin.
Santa Croce at Florence has basso relievo tombstones on floor. Ruskin admired the two near door.

Earthquake shock at Genoa day after we left. Had a description of one there by an American.

Large yellow fiery, star in the East end window of St. Peter's.

The name of "Silvestre" distinctly written on the stone of the names of the streets of ancient Rome, in the museum on the Capitol. Wolf raging to & fro in a café half way up the ascent.

Very wearied today, Sunday, could scarcely drag back to lodging. Not much sleep lately, noise of the streets & fountain kept me awake last night. Narrow escape first day we drove out, a waggon & two horse lost control of, our driver turned off into side street.

Procession of red-gowned men

through streets often

Uncomfortable quarters at Hôtel Bologna, hard bed, noisy square, & b—gs, noise of fountain as well as traffic, the latter as great as Londons   No sleep.

The impressiveness of the stupendous ruins of the Palatine hill & the Forum overpowering – quite easy to realize the life in rooms where the decorations were still distinct   One festooned with wreaths of flowers; a portrait figure subject in other, salon, & salle à manger amphorae hanging at entrance, portions of tiled floor & marble etc.

Picked up bit of marble on the steps of temple of Jupiter on the Palatine hill – Monday 27. I was very used up & rather ill on getting out of bed – very weak & miserable through Monday & Tuesday

Tuesday came to Hôtel Allemagne.[55] I rested in afternoon. Tom went out & nearly lost himself trying to find baths of Caracalla & dragged about.

Wednesday I felt well – Tom rather weak, had a nice day, fine weather. Warmer   Went to Vatican saw a part the picture portion & Sistine Chapel   Had lunch volaille gelantine at the restaurant as before – curtains there drawn up in festoons quite short like a Valance. & a pinkish purplish tint in the glass of the window – a vault or cellar-like place, gave one a chill to sit long there.

In the afternoon strolled about up the Corso & in an omnibus to the bridge of St. Angelo. Then back again to the Forum, sat on ledges & walls regarding it. & looked at shops, people ruins, traffic, all the rest of the time.

I felt quite strong again & able to enjoy it

Immense traffic on the bridge   Chiefly carts of building materials

Much building going on in Rome   Houses torn down everywhere.[56]

Building materials carried about in rough carts with mules, poor little things too small & too heavily laden, so that when a drove comes along, the efforts of men & mules are distressing, & obstructive.

Met the American (Jerusalem family) who said he would meet us at Rome & he did, in the Corso about 4 o'clock.

Afterwards went to the Capitol again too late for the Tabularium or vaults with antiquities & staircase down to the Forum. Walked down the steps of the Capitol where the wolves are, after Tom had been to see the Tarpeian Rock, went into a picture shop, bought a picture, Tom walked with it along a narrow street St. Marco. The attack by confederate thieves dreadful fright to me – got into an omnibus & back to hotel –[57]

Thursday. Went to Colosseum driving there, then to English cemetery visiting Shelley & Keats' grave, strolled about under the Triumphal Arches, after lunch,. Walked about & went in omnibus & bought another picture at same shop.

Girls coming into dinner in hats, etc speaking fluent Italian.

Cart horses, have a bundle of straw or hay close to their heads.

The road to the English Cemetery

via St. Paolo,

Streets paved with small stones large lozenge-shaped stones alone marking the pavement [SKETCH] & a dip in the centre for rain to run off into. So that they soon dry up. New & wide streets have pavements.

Gathered violets off graves of Shelley & Keats.[58] Lovely cemetery very full Crowded where Shelley is, his grave up in a place by itself, a quiet corner but not a pretty one, & old door behind. The cemty. is hilly & well planted. Camelia tree in full bloom of crimson flowers.

Words on grave-stone very pathetic
Here lies Keats who in the bitterness of his heart & mind etc.[59]

Strings of bladders hanging up at provision shops.

Beggars standing with their backs bent against leathern curtains at Church doors. You see the curtain bent outwards so that you can pass in at the side, & then you percei[ve] the man – who instantly begs & remains as before till the service is over.

An omnibus contains a variety of people, priests nuns, girls without bonnets English & American young ladies etc. – the nun who was fat placed her large cross carefully prominent on her lap – though handkerchiefs are much worn on heads, often old people with grey or no hair scarcely go without – always gay colours worn –

Had two nice letters for Tom from Kegan Paul & Gosse about Woodlanders[60] [*Wednesday?*]

Little potatoes economically used

at table d'hôte in dishes of stewed beef with onions same size & bits of carrot, all size of marble. Nothing like a big hotel for studying economy.

A great many dangers in Rome streets. So much building going & materials carried along, nearly had something down upon us from scaffolding at Capitol

Italian boys begging or selling, say "Peak English, get away, get away" in a pleading tone not knowing the meaning.

Plenty of blue sky now we have got to Rome.

The room of the Philosophers in the museum of the Capitol is rather droll, these innumerable heads in every attitude of meditation & variety of solemn expression.

Wife of Hadrian in one room very

stately & beautiful.

The great down-bed coverlet not found at ordinary hotels, we had a huge one at Aix les Bains, & one bed. But white counterpanes, & two narrow bed like hospital beds at Florence, also at Rome. No blankets in beds at Rome hotel Bologna (a wretched place) Only coarse sheets & a thick quilted counterpane & a white one, flock pillow

At Hôtel Allemagne, a large nice one Scarlet carpet, white forc-post iron bedstead covered with muslin curtains the same at Genoa − − A green curtain at door with two cord pulleys to draw.

Most droves of oxen carts on the Via Paola going to Cemetery, patient sad eyed creatures − ropes round horns as harness, large well fed animals

Think of Florence as home from here.

Looked at Ruins over again today. Feel we know the Forum & Colosseum   Shops in narrow streets are always square holes in wall with no wood work, often, generally, no doors, always open for vegetables & provisions –

Large butcher's shops like ours – Plenty of furniture shops in old streets

Venus in Museum at Capitol left hand side; she stands in a large recess like a chapel, her hand touches her right thigh, fingers being spread our naturally both little toes crumpled under as if she had worn boots.

Infant Hercules, superbly childish in face & thick in limbs

Friday April 1st.[61]

Vatican 2nd. time – to see sculptures. Drove in cab, after much worrying whether we should go again or not. Fine day, but cold. At 12.30, after lunching at the cellar-like restaurant as usual – we started from the hotel an intelligent driver being hired by the doorporter, & got to the Catacombs. After an hour there, drove a long way on the Via Appia, then back, & turned off in another direction, reached hotel before six o'clock, walked out bought photographs, & had coffee in Corso, a large restaurant up steps, looked on garden arrangement for summer.

Catacombs astonishing, so extensive, so winding, so earthy – Ventilated right up through to the

gardens, market gardens flourishing above
them – a very singular experience. Several
storeys – We crept through one turning, have
to bend & the sides all earthy touching our
elbows. The guide a monk Capuchins, one of
those clothed in cream coloured flannel, under
his dark lower garment he wore trousers of
the same white flannel, he was amused at our
repugnance, very garrulous, relating whole
legends of saints, especially St. Cecilia. Glass
case for mummy & skeleton dust of bones &
white bits of bone distinguishable amongst
dust.

A place which filled one with sorrow &
gloom, sorrow at the thought of the misery,
endured by the persecuted Xtians

when in hiding here. We seemed like magnified ants burrowing under ground as we walked –

Guide carried a coil of wax taper round his stick, & cut off a length for me, when I asked him what I should do, mine having burnt low down.

Square chambers frequently, with better tombs – one of sculptured marble to an Irishman O'Connell[62]

Grease about everywhere.

The monk who received us & got us to write our names in his book, quite a remarkable man. Tall, quaint with a fine head. Very polite bowing profoundly to me as he waved me to the way on.

On first entering, it seemed an adventure & it was impossible to help feeling a sensation of horror at the bare chance of being left behind, as one caught glimpses of innumerable dark windings, all precisely alike, & interminable.

Singular effect, through an archway when another party appeared suddenly with torches & then passed on –

Glad to see daylight at last.

The drive equally astonishing   The sides of the road, which were as wide as the sides of a Cornish road, lined the whole way with tombs, some of them mere heaps of stones, others with scraps of ornament, a few with a façade sufficiently well preserved to enable one easily to comprehend how magnificent this Way once was with handsome edifices to the dead like those in Père la Chaise – occasionally a torso, or a head of marble rested against a tomb – but not often.

A wealthy family were visiting one tomb (of their ancestors).

Saturday. Stayed on a day longer. Mrs. Baxter was to come Sunday but sent a telegram to say she couldn't

Drove to St. Peters' in Montorio church. Saw spot where his cross stood. A little hole in floor of small chapel. Priest took up earthy sand & gave it to us.[63] Bought photographs Very tired   Rested afternoon   Taken a cold from yesterday's drive.

Sunday. T.H. went to St. Paul's early
Palm Sunday – Saw people kissing statue of
St. Peter – (Little statues of a sitting St. Peter
sold in shops)   I got up later & posted card to
sister – & walked a little. Left at 11. am –
French lady, German lady in train   French
one left, & our first acquaintance got in,
strange coincidence, we had travelled from
London Holborn Station –

Reached Florence at 7.[64] Wet day, had
cleared. Mrs & Mr Macnamee came in to see
us when we were dining in little room. Large
bedroom in another part of house.

Saw clouds lying low on mountains
Amiata <St. Marello [sic]> quite near us. The
clouds were caught as it were – the Arno,
today a lovely blue. With a dash of opal in it.
Below sparking & foaming

over rocks like a Devonshire river a great contrast to the Yellow Tiber.

Gentleman & little child in train.

Sweet voice, baby Italian   Speech very attractive – very noisy & playful.

Florence more backward in vegetation than Rome & wetter

The foliage appearing round Rome   A few people at work in vineyards

All crops coming up, & earth freshly turned.

Felt very feverish on train; my yesterday's cold rather worse.[65]

Hotels dearer in Rome but a half franc goes further there with porters etc than in Florence.

Market women from the country quite plainly dressed. The gaily attired women & children, in streets of Rome offering flowers, & thrusting them in your face, or leaving them on your arm till they fall off, then darting under people's feet to get them again — are Neapolitans. They are [*unnerving?*]

[SKETCH] Few or no hedges in country Very low ones sometimes, or [SKETCH] rails. Few plantations of trees, few large trees, acres & acres of vine growing cultivated fields.

The Evangelist at Hotel, always busy, telling visitors what to see,

At breakfast this morning, related his experience & difficulty in getting an orderly "audience" Congregation he meant

Monday morning, Breakfasted in little room with Lady who had stayed more than a year in Rome & told me of the subterranean ways and aqueducts. Then to the church & monastery of St. Marco.

The cells quite fair-sized chambers seeming very possible to live comfortably in – Savonarola's face, like Fanny W's wife & still more like George Eliot. A long face, nose, & massive jaw.

His hair shirt; (twisted hair like small cord woven) his flannel under gown & black over dress all in a cabinet hung against the wall.

A convenient desk under the glass part, his written books, very minute hand-writing – much marginal writing, lined in red ink.

Curious effect to see all the cells empty. & the waxen effigy of one in a glass case. An old fact with toothless jaws. Outside in corridor, a long dark wood bench with high back.

A beautiful cloister with frescoes in still brilliant colours by Fra Angelico

In a room by itself the large picture of the crucifixion   The effect of the glorias round their head was exactly like straw hats, put on because they were out of doors –

Two cruc‡fixes, one Xt. dying & the blood streaming down the other – dead –

Called on Mrs. Baxter afternoon. A Mrs. Craik[66] & daughters there. & Priest & little priest blessing the house & taking wine.

Took pencil sketch of bridge.
Better native shops here than in

Rome. Native shops there either copper utensils or provision shops with bladders of lard, the colour of mahogany hung up over the door with polonies & other such things, like a fringe, & very low so as to touch heads or nearly –

Flower girls & boys pester one more in Rome, Lovely baskets of flowers at shop doors & corners there.

Everyone welcomes us here in this pension – especially the American family (Jerusalems)   Met mother & son on stairs   Interesting family.

Our bedroom has a terrace, very pretty. Scarlet velvet chairs & long settee going all along wall. No lovely cats in Italy as in France   'All short hair ones.

The fresco of "Xt welcomed by monks" in Savonarola's monastery is miserable I think. I like the other frescoes there, & I like those at St. Giovanni's in Lateran & those of St. Assisi in St. Croce Florence seem to have been beautiful once. But old frescoes are horrid entre-nous (Note-book & I).

Tuesday, make sketches in morning

Drove to the monastery of Certosa   Had a liqueur glass & green & white wine Chartreuse. Suite of apartments for monk with garden each. Exquisite views from little terrace. Very high situation   Rosemary & red anemonies growing in large garden with cloisters round, merry monk, <u>two</u>, lay brothers. Large number of visitors. Fine chapels.

Effigy of abbot on floor of one & pictures by Fra Angelico.

The Pope's rooms (Sixtus): confined here by Napoleon because he refused

162 *Diary 3*

dispensation of dissolution of N's marriage.

Thursday – went to Pictures Belli Arti. Triptychs, old, with gilded backgrounds

<u>Devils</u> in large picture of Last Judgement – Fra Angelico – marvellously horrible & active in tormenting.

Met first travelling acquaintance there.

<u>David</u> by Michael Angelo, a huge statue – quite nude but nothing art – distinctive – fine limbs

Bought "Dante" in afternoon   Wet weather. Felt sad at having left Rome. No ruins to go to here.

Copies of Roman statuary –

Sellers of embroideries – & nick-nacks in hall of pension daily.

Flower girls of Rome – quite an institution; nothing like so numerable here.

The mountain caught up clouds which we
see coming from Rome here is called Amiata
[SKETCH]

The one seen from the convent on the hill is
Santa Morello [*sic*]

Thursday. Cathedral service with a procession of priests in gorgeous vestments
carrying the baldaquin with host beneath
through the aisles. Throngs of people. One
old priest gazing too.

Went in afternoon with Mrs Baxter shopping (grocer etc)   Afterwards to studio. Mr
Parks an American.

Then to make a call on a Mrs. Griffiths an
artist's widow, & a lady friend. An officer in
full uniform there: Room like an ordinary
English room splendid view of mountains
close to it.

The house behind our pension

Fire distinctly to be seen in the acolytes' censors. Blazing up occasionally –

<Mrs Simpson's sister (widowed) in Jerusalem>

Mrs Simpson – daughter – <u>rich</u> of Mars family. Other girl is cousin.

We call them the Jerusalem family because of their adventure –

Mrs Griffiths' house like well got up houses in London. <u>Plants & plush</u>

T.H. got up at 5. & started for Sienna.

Artist colour shops have [SKETCH] splashes of colour on the window as sign board.

[SKETCH]   Provision shops in Rome hung with puddings

Read Reviews in Library   Good Friday morning. Drove & walked to eminence. Ch. S. Miniato al Monte & cemetery   Exquisite views. Made sketch   Church in three parts – body, crypt & gallery. Transparent marble windows. Encrusted marble work screen. Round pillars of mottled marble   Very lovely tombs on floor, with crosses & immortelles easy to stumble over. Very old church in exterior. Large cemetery, tombs like Père La Chaise   Grand

Saturday. Miss Preston called. Went to English Cemetery to see Mrs Browning's[67] grave, only EBB on it – not a pretty cemetery

Saw a concourse of people, country folks largely, at the Cathedral. The Dove & Fireworks show. Very cold evening.

Green, bright & very bright persiennes to all windows. Dark blue & indigo mountains

Arno, varies in colour daily – houses chiefly yellow, buff rather, tinted to almost white – russet & brown roofs – straight low & having structures like observatories on top –

Italian voices not sweet, the gabble no prettier than any other language, but the street calls striking in their vowel enunciation.
[SKETCH]   Dark brown cheeses –

Easter Sunday. St. Annunciata church crowded. Mostly standing. Splendid singing solos. Brass wind instruments. Organs, one looking like a monument – played a few full loud strains now & then – very near us. During a lull in service at high altar – the murmuring of priests voice heard at the other end of church where the sacrament was being taken in a little structure surrounded by swinging bronze lamps lit with tiny flames like those at the tomb of St. Peter at Rome.

Called on Mrs Baxter, Miss Preston, Dodge & then on Miss Paget[68]   Her brother handsome & full faced lying on a couch covered with a cloth, 11 years a sufferer from spinal complaint. Miss Paget, gentle & different from London style of her. Loves the country   Is snubbed by her   Is miserable in London. Had tea both places.

Mrs Simpson gave me a large bunch of lilies of the valley & Mrs Macnamee a rose. The table & room profusely adorned with flowers. Also the churches on this Easter Sunday in Flower-ence.

Monday   Uffizi gallery again morning
afternoon – with Mrs. Baxter to Fiesole
– Accident – Reception at Miss Pagets in
evening. Saw her father – mother & brother
ill. Madame Hill. English & naturalised Flor-
entine. Very friendly – Signor [*blank space*]
who reads English literature & speaks a little
English. Miss Sargent who sketches & is
drawing from models at school of art here.
Miss Preston. Miss Dodge, others.

Tuesday. Very much worn out   Both of
us utterly prostrate. Invited to lunch with
Miss Paget & her invalid brother. Took leave
of Mrs Baxter & went shopping.

Wednesday 12.

Came to Venice.[69] Hôtel Angleterre
Went out again in a gondola & one man, up
the Grand Canal.

First view of Venice from train, is enchanting in its beauty & novelty. Marshes appear first then more & more water & the city white & glorious a little way off –

The first sight of Gondolas as cabs waiting to take us to hotel novel

The cab journey through the streets strangest sensation – then the sight of the palaces, stately, a silent rowing. The shooting under low arched bridges – or standing on the bridges & seeing the gondolas passing with a glide under one's feet. The blue sky & glassy green clear sea-weedy water   The yellow & white edifices with sunlight on them – deep narrow gully streets – then the startling Piazza of St. Marco with the sun blazing on its gilded front.[70]

The large space in front so unexpected, & the beautiful architecture on all four sides of arcaded palaces all remarkable –

Quaint old hotel – Ropes up the passages for bannisters – not otherwise remarkable. T.H. cross at finding we are not on Grand Canal & our Jerusalem friends are at Hotel Swiss

Friday 15. Very wet day. Went out a little while. Bought a pr of shoes & fed pigeons in Piazza. Had exhibition of lace-purchases in bedroom after dinner. About £2 for 1 handkerchief Venetian point.

[DOODLE]   Very fatigued with yesterday.

Yesterday met the Jerusalem family, women morning, Mr Mars Jun. in Piazza evening. Went to St Marks church & galleries, & then to Island San Giorgio Maggiore's church with carved figures in choir & Campanile view.

Saturday evening – Singers at dinner time outside – very harmonious – Cold wintry weather – went to Belli Arti – A picture of Madonna with St. Cathr. & Mary Mag – by Bellini (Giovanni). The infant just the right expression. Sadness & astonishment   The only one I have ever seen with this –

Porters & men wear blue blouses in Venice as in France. Dialect soft.

Pictures of St. Mark doing many things One – coming down from heaven to save a slave   Another – coming with St. Nicholas & another to save Venice from a hurricane & a demon ship.

A kind of green moss growing up between pavement stones – Wells & chains & bucket copper ones in some of the little squares Campi

Shawls of every dirty colour old & shabby worn, over shoulders & sometimes heads, often nothing even in rainy weather on heads – of poor people – dowdy – all of them unlike other Italian cities –

Lots of English shops. Here & everywhere

Occasionally a gaily dressed woman with tiara of beads on her head & large horn behind her head.

Sunday saw the Doge's palace[71] & prisons – three holes for blood to run away where they were strangled – door to throw them into boat tied into sack – taken away to the sea

"I have long wished to be recalled to your benevolent remembrance & could find no pleasanter reminder than Mr. Thomas Hardy the novelist who is going with Mrs. Hardy to Venice for a little while. Now no one has seen Venice thoroughly who has not been to Casa Alvisi. I need say no more. (I hear that you have sent us back poor Henry James quite ill, what a shame (My best remembrances to Miss Bronson & believe me yours truly – (Miss P's letter)[72]

Casa Alvisi – S Maria del Figlio

I know I am doing you a pleasure while doing my friends a service in introducing to you Mr & Mrs Thomas Hardy. You who appreciate the charm of Mr. Hardy's novels & the additional value they give to our country life, will be able better than anyone to give Mr Hardy & his wife the means of appreciating Venice. I shall write at greater length as soon as my plans are settled – (Another) Mrs Curtis[73]

Monday – Covered gondola to Ghetto. Gondolier pleased at our admiration. Walks round on ledge to clean it whilst T.H. was gone – Fine old palace with wide entrance from water – door with pediments then on right double columned entrance to square court with well in centre. Stone balustraded gallery above. Two storeys. Some of them missing – narrow passages & stairs, & grated windows at kitchens round this court. On other side of entrance hall stone benches about a wide staircase. At other end of it a square, public with well, the people passing through the entrance, up the stairs, or to the water entrance, where a little street serves continually. Up stairs great old wooden doors bound with iron & marble portals. A school in one room, & a gorgeous painted ceiling contrasting with the bare benches & a wooden partition forming a living room. Another door led into an ante-room   A picture in ceiling, remains of frescoes on wall – a small room seen through a chink all gorgeous with frescoes & rich ceiling – Then a carpenter's work room – men at work   Gorgeous painted ceiling-piece of timber resting against portrait of lady – against her Venetian point-lace bertha, sleeves matched velvet gown – their hats & coats on pegs on a frame resting against portrait of gentleman. Pathetic to see them thus degraded, apparently the original possessors. Melancholy to see so much marble & decoration dropping to decay.

Whilst in the gondola – a troop of women passed along on left side, coming from work – every one had a shawl over her head & though not gay, the mass with deep blues purples, every shade of brown & occasionally green looked rich & odd   [SKETCH]

Afternoon resting – my knee being jointless. T.H. has taken letters of Int: to the ladies – Very disappointing for me – (For the best always)

Evening. Gondola to the Rialto back by Sospiri   Water brilliant as sky dotted with stars of light & reflections, wavering as if loth to go into black deps & receding to light again   Vessel full of Chinese lamps & singers going silently like a magic ship – then motionless before a palace, then bursting into noise. Violin, guitars & voices

In the harbour the effect of lights & edifices like the harbour at Devonport rather, but on the G. Canal like nothing   Essence of poetical beauty. Stillness, only the splash of the oar – which echoes under bridges – I light in centre of the Rialto   This seems not wide enough <u>beneath</u> to contain three divisions & shops & <u>steps</u> above it – Resting the gondola is quite motionless. Stars innumerable & very bright. Then gliding into the narrow canals, though lighted here & there – seems dark & dangerous & very dark places continually beyond, & to pass, shoot under narrow bridges, the gondolier shouting a warning note before he turns sharply round each corner – primé or stati, according as he goes in opposite direction – if he goes stati he calls "left" to the other who may be coming. Nobody comes generally – but he shouts each time –

The post office is an anomaly – How can it be one up in a corner of a water-lane – steps down to the water looks absurd, odd – anything. In fact, the whole city makes one feel fantastic, or beyond. Romantic. You are in a planet, where things are managed differently, or you are gone to the bottom of the sea, & this is a phantom city, or you are simply dreaming –

The solemnest darkest & most dangerous looking is past this again into narrower ways where barges are lying like black dragons guarding strange gloomy entrances, then on under Ponte Dei Sospiri. Bridge of sighs. Dark palace with a gleam of light on it, on right hand side, darker prison on the other, where a door, horrible to see, appears, a low ordinary door. This is the spot. The dreadful sack appeared – thrown into the boat [SKETCH]

The steps are both ways, gondolier steps

out first & draws gondola to second steps
[SKETCH]   Beggar-man tonight got us into gondola & we thought he was gondolier all the time till he held out his hat in the usual way – They speak a word or two of English.

The Lions' Mouth in Doges Palace is only a hole in wall of ante room one side & a locked box in the other room. The room which has a doorway carved & protruding into the room in a corner – Two passages through it – one to a good room, the other narrow winding leading to stairs & an iron door beneath to the prisons on the leads & prisons (?) below –

Traces in plaster of wall show the size of the Lion's head, which has evidently been removed –

Some men perhaps police – wear long gowns of blue with white bands round waists. Walking in the streets –

Boccaccio's house halfway down the hill from <u>Fiesole</u>. Mrs B. pointed it out.

Canova's at Rome in a back street (?)   It appeared to be his by fragments & figures & inscriptions.

None of the Campaniles quite perpendicular   Numerous buildings out of it – walls are all or nearly all in the narrow alleys in a bulging state, & crumbling, many timbers rotting   One old house with very broken timbers –

Pillars of white marble all in one piece in Church of S. Maria della Salute. Also in Degli Scalzi (?)   Carved figures reposing in the choir of [*S. Maria della Salute*]   Went to three churches Tuesday – I felt better. T.H. toothache.

Carved choir wormeaten. Inlaid wood in Frari. Brown monks in Scalzi spoke

English or anything visitors did enquiring first. Showed the marble with rapid repetition. Jasper. Striped reds like book lining verd d'antique. Like green cloth thrown about. Black Norwegian. White Carrara –

Picture of Madonna by Bellini in Sacristy of S. Maria Salute – considered good. I unable to appreciate it – liked the saints at side better – like fishermen.

Old palaces have a large &˙long entrance hall with doors – staircase, writer's room – gates to water, outercourt with well & entrance gate to street or square at back, colonnades sometimes, varied, but this is general plan.

White stockings. Bad colour large feet invariable with the poor & poorest.

Foscari Palace, very plain inside & different from others, having its court & garden, (door to be seen & well, a very old, worn, one) with handsome windows & balcony looking into it, all at the street entrance, & no colonnades, few doors, a plain staircase only inside – Red & handsome on the water frontage –

Glass shop & mosaics – Four men required for a month to make one figure full length in mosaic. Two men employed in preparing squares of coloured glass & stone, with rapidly revolving wheels & water, grinding them smooth – Two others called artists fitting in pieces on soft grey mortar, a very little at a time, a lump the size of a hand on table with bits – fitting them in like a puzzle.

Frari Church – numerous monuments one of Canova [SKETCH] pyramid & weeping figures & lion

Enormous tomb to a patriot – colossal figures next to Canovas – People reading guides aloud close to worshippers after bell has rung too – two sacristies – very rich screen & carved choir. Old picturesque beggar stood in centre of church [SKETCH] Wide cloak & hat [SKETCH] held in hand   Long chains to lamps hanging from roof all brass swinging. Broken window on high – dilapidated church – the very bell for elevation · of <u>host</u> was cracked

Uneven floor in St Marco   These three churches we saw today Tuesday 19 April – almost weary of seeing churches & beggars Bronze little statues standing in fonts.

Fine converging pavement under dome at S. Mari della Salute plain interior. Fine old pictures in all churches.

Font in crypt of Fiesole church was formerly used for wine at feast of Bacchus.

Piazza St. Marco resembles Palais Royale a little

April 20. Shopped morning finding my way through the intricate alleys to the Rialto & back to Schiavoni   Visited ladies Mrs. Curtis in Palazzo Barbarossi & Mrs. Bronson in Casa Vecchia

Old lady with gold chain to eye-glasses & nice old gentleman looking ahead, find suite of rooms with stucco walls large decorative paintings on walls, fine ceilings with pictures   Old palace – good state, fine view of canal in front – well furnished Maple style – & with Liberty combined & Venetia ornaments thrown in. Decoration for festival ⌐ Lion of St. Mark on crimson silk stretched on a board. Shown to us   Portraits of former proprietors hanging in anti room, copies by artist's son of originals

Entered from side canal, gondolier of their own acting as servant took our card up – long flight of steps to house –

Rather a mean entrance

2 House. Way through an ill-smelly winding narrow way – Too early – turned away to return later   Met lady at entrance – Cordial lively woman – little Venetian dog. Met her at foot of stairs – gondolier opened door again – dressed a trifle like sailor   Collar & dark blue trousers & jacket   She writes plays for private, 4 persons.

Countess Morini[74] – Venetian belle came Lovely eyes, fine complexion, brown & buff dress   V. fine feathered hat, brown gloves Lovely green plust jacket – Mrs. B in a nice grey dress, black plush mantle lined with gold satin – Gondolier handed her – Countess helped herself to more, wrote her name in T. H.'s notebook & was very affable & simple – has a baby & a nurse   One of the fine race of nurse.

Countess walked round the room looking at things as she admires the taste of her English friend & copies: with her tea cup in left hand held steady, & her sunshade a reddish silk with deep red handle & silver filigree top like a walking stick – tucked under her right arm – too valuable to be left about evidently

Thursday – Lunched at Barbarossa Palace with Mr & Mrs Curtis & Mr Brown   Picture of Venetian girl by Sargent hanging opposite me at dinner – painter a relative perhaps. Flower in tall vase in centre chiefly red anemones flanked by little glasses of primroses – grey-headed man servant very attentive with the wine particularly, waited. Not gondolier   Flatfish, then Italian dish like macaroni pudding but not that. Slices of meat pudding. Every thing handed twice   Coffee in drawing room after. Mr. Curtis took me because it was a long way – four or five rooms. All well furnished. Mrs Curtis' bedroom looking on canal & very pretty.

Walked about in afternoon   Went into church   Cat came to me 5th cat in Italy across nave. Tom & Mrs Bronson came in – walked about with her

Went to dinner with her at 7.30   Mr Eden acting as host took me in – Lame, walked with two sticks, had to be arranged upon chairs at table – a libertine-looking man. The <u>Montalbas</u>   Heard singing from lighted barge on the canal, sitting on the balcony – The boat a pretty object – lit with Chinese lanterns Gondolas gliding up & remaining stationary   Others darting swiftly & silently about. Some at a distance – stars – No other sound except a rival singing, clear female voice – no steamers at night   Strange experience to sit with English friends on the balcony of a Venetian Palace on Grand Canal at night & listen to singing of gondoliers or

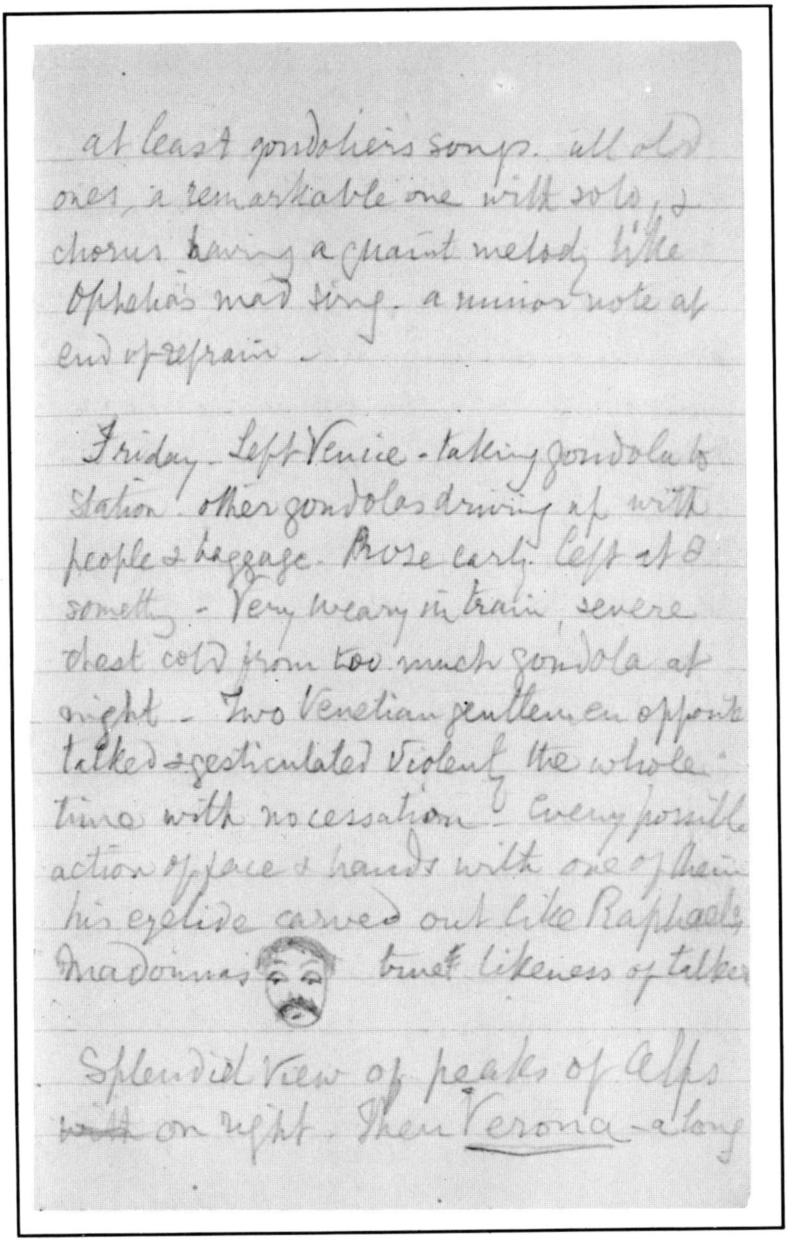

at least gondoliers' songs. All old ones, a remarkable one with solo & chorus having a quaint melody like Ophelia's mad song – a minor note at end of refrain.

Friday[75] – Left Venice. Taking gondola to station. Other gondolas driving up with people & luggage. Rose early. Left at 8 something. Very weary in train, severe chest cold from too much gondola at night. Two Venetian gentlemen opposite talked & gesticulated violently the whole time with no cessation. Every possible action of face & hands with one of them his eyelids carved out like Raphaels Madonnas [SKETCH] True likeness of talker

Splendid view of peaks of Alps on right. Then Verona. A long

stretch of city & Alps behind. Red roofs,
towers, etc. Looked a pretty & an interesting
place. { Romeo & }
        { Juliet   }

Young Scotchman fellow traveller. Home
from India. Came to Milan about 4 o'clock.
Had tea in Cafée at half-past – & went into the
Cathedral – an immense enormous structure.[76] Columns surmounted with niches &
statues instead of ordinary capitols. Brass line

in floor – (Meridian)

Hôtel Grand de Milan – very large with
complete electric arrangements & long salon à
manger   T.H. went to see the Bridge of
Lodi, with companion[77] – I went about Milan
– took trains   Second, took me so far that I
was not back in time to meet Tom for lunch.
Went out again at three o'clock to top of roof
of Cathedral

Marvellous profusion of marble statues & decorations, flying buttresses, crocketted pinnacles & marble steps

Man selling photographs of views of roof & from it, living all day up there   You can get near enough to some of the statues & tracery to put your hand upon it & little Cherubins are damaged by ruthless visitors. Every bit has been carefully carved behind & in corners, profuse & unsparing work. St. Sebastian pink marble with his skin wrapped round his body after flaying, horribly natural – face quite small, expression agony & horror – Names under each statue – & every person of note in the land there – Felt fear by myself so descended rapidly – lest I should meet any rough person – Then I

bought necktie for Henry.[78] Fan, for self –
then took open carriage for $1\frac{1}{2}$ franc & told the
driver who spoke French, to take me to the
principal Churches. He evidently liked the
idea. Saint Sepulchro was the most singular.
In each aisle there was a representation in
coloured statuary life size, & exactly like life in
every particular most striking – Christ with
robe & crown of thorns mocked. The other
Christ at Pharisee's supper having his feet
washed by M. Magdalene   This the best.
The company at the table excited & natural,
the hand of one at the right of spectator held
out pointing, so that you could take hold of it
it was so near you.

Drove back after seeing 5

or 6 to Hotel. T & I went out to dine at Restaurant. Left at 7.30 for Lucerne.

Came through Mt. St. Gothard. The loveliest scenery & a wonderful journey – Lake of Como, stopping at station 5 minutes, then seeing it from train a glassy piece of water, reflection of surrounding mountains – houses nestled close, young spring foliage – slight trees, mountains behind Mountains loveliest colours everywhere, an enchanting spot.[79] Then on up the mountains through numerous tunnels Cascades & mountains Streams Snow on top of mountains Higher yet higher, up amongst the snow at last, very astonishing, not cold – I wretched, miserable with severe cold caught at Venice

190   *Diary 3*

All the windows open. Travellers excited at scenery. A family with 3 restless children, ill-trained.

Mountain streams turned into rivers as we came down the other side, foaming over boulders.

Scenery quite changed – Swiss chalets.

A walk or drive all along the border of Zug

– (?) a lovely lake.

Fertile plains – lovely village   Very green grass – red roofs always.

<When we came from Milan we saw> Verona – a large picturesque extending town, very long streets

Today we saw Rigi, & the one carriaged train going there

Lots of primroses on the way to Como, in fields & banks –

Milan a Paris without the interesting edifices – fine wide streets, good shops – & a handsome place for promenade – Gallerie de Victor Emmanuel – I did not care for it – but an excellent contrast after Venice[80] – so civilized & horses & carriages to be seen nice more

– Reached Lucerne 5 o'clock Sunday[81] – fine weather all journey – gleams of sunshine on large place – this Lucerne

Tom is gone out – I rest here being so miserable with a cold

Better in afternoon – Tom & I walked about – climbed a hill Sat in the sun by a Pension looking down on lake

Walked by the side of lake before in morning a short walk – saw a diagram marked on a marble pedestal, of all the mountains – & the Rigi very distinct to the left. In some places, the town looks a little like Venice, where the houses are close to the water – Walked through one covered bridge, saw the other. Very old, clumsy & curious having painted each side of triangle in roof made by cross-beams – up very high |SKETCH| The wounded Lion cut in rock very good –

Some trouble to get into a carriage for Paris. Tom & the father of family (3 little ones) who had travelled with us thither – had an altercation. Then we left him master of it, & got into another – Changed at Basle – gentleman apologised for not getting out for me – & seemed really sorry – no doubt out of gratitude for my taking his part, & pitying his trying situation with the children.

Reached Paris Tuesday morning about 7. Only boots & one man up at the Albert Hotel Rue St Hyacinthe St. Honoré – Ill with diarrhoea as I was coming – Slept tolerably in train, till I felt this – Another husband & wife – French people, came after we had left 3 stations out of Basle   A gentleman had come before & some rustics from a fair evidently; got in at Basle & left at next station

Mem. I don't like a pillow unless we are alone & can stretch out, also seems odd when there's another man.

Walked about Paris. Saw the Crown Jewels exhibited before their sale   A queue formed – a crowd of people

Splendid jewels – guarded by men inside a circle which surrounded the glass case   They were under an enormous one – officials very numerous, making us pass quickly round it & on. The room a very large one hung with crimson silk curtains & draperies, with tables & seats for the sale – A dome of crimson raised over the case of jewels – People let into building by batches –

Went to café, walked, bought photograph – took a long drive in the Rivoli and about the city

The Tuileries quite disappeared. An iron temporary erection. The effect on me – of this disappearance, the gardens left in their stately grandeur & the jewels for sale, was very saddening –

April 27. Arrived in London at 7 P.M. after a rough but fine passage.

Diary 4

The Visit to Switzerland

June–July 1897

Switzerland June 1897

June 15. Left Max Gate for Southampton[82] Slept on board the Columbia. Calm sea. Lovely night.

16. Arrived at Havre. Sunshiny day.
Tall trees – poplars – like dressed poles in rows helping out a few hedges to divide the patches of tillage – travelled all day – drove through Paris, came to

Dijon – Hotel de Jura – Fine cat sitting on stand in entrance: Finely painted ceilings Cold weather.

17. Pontarlier – very pretty little girl, a German in train. Friendly.

Coupé carriage – fine scenery – single line.

18. Neuchâtel – Hôtel de Lac. White curtained beds. Narrow salon. Through Bureau Armoury very fine in Bureau. Town surrounded by mountains. Cold. Rainy – stormy – a square in front & an Hotel – We had come through tunnels in the Jura. Set our watches an hour on –) <Tapestry & seats there on first floor landing> Small pretty little port with vessels

French lady opposite at Déjeuner   Horrid
man by   Wrote postcards – Deep blue
distance – Went out by edge of Lac – stormy –
the stone table plan two inches in rain. T.H.
disliked the rain & cold.

19. Berne. Hôtel Belle Vue
Beautiful scenery – bridges – distant mountains – but misty weather – could not see them
– only to be seen occasionally   Fine Cathedral terrace – steep slopes streets hilly – town
lying partly below our hotel the garden with
fine view – like the Terrace   High place also
just outside with same view: no view from
our windows. Streets with deep massive
arcades. Broad streets – fountains at intervals
– Market day we left. Dogs in carts. The River
Aar

20. Wet. Sunday. I went to English Cathedral. Almost all Protestants – a novelty when
one travels. A very small Roman Catholic Ch.
Wonderful clock with

brass running round. Bears – everywhere the Bären Live bears in a den – I fed them with the other people. Idle men lounging Stalls for sale of carved things Festival service in evening at Cathedral. Niggers voices – Black women with unearthly fine voice. "Oh yes" song. Much wanted fine weather.

21. Weather clearing – We walked to the Schangli – (a lady I met told me)   Had tea. Lovely scenery. Mountains   Nice place. Large. Tea. Birds' warbling – a cat. Long walk – lost new spectacles.

22. June – Jubilee.[83] Brilliant Day. After dull & wet. Many English in Hôtel (Belle-vue)   Breakfast & out before T.H. up.

Went to see the Bear's Den – walked through the market – in streets – &-all-round-Cathedral. Went on to

Interlaken. Hotel Metro-pole. First near view of Jungfrau from window (see sketch) seen over lovely garden & gay street

Mountains all round Jungfrau were white all day. Pink glow morning & night[84] Exquisite like a bride – Pretty walks with trees. Seats, band, beautiful sunshine on snow. Lovely country walks – the sweetest place of all, & we cheerful again

Wed. 23. Very fine weather   Drove to the Grindelwald, boy brushing flies off horse with a branch – train parallel. Bridges mountains – river – [*space*]. Saw – the three mountains – Wetterhorn. Eiger   Mönch   Got into train – left carriage – Went up the Wengern Alp. Extraordinary   Higher & higher – at last banks of snow on either side – enormous glaciers   To change trains got out at Medeeck [*sic*]. Instead of getting into another walked across the Wengern Alp (path being repaired).[85] Gathered flowers   The blue Gentian   Large blue violets. Not sweet. Daisies – buttercups   Lots of wild parsley about in Switzerland

everywhere. Hot superb day – Tea – lots of people. Hotel restaurant outside seats & tables
Sitting on Railway bank. Waiting for train   Luggage trains coming to hotel Looking at Jungfrau Eiger etc – Nearly an avalanche   Clouds descending on mountains – Just then fat German fell as he caught his wife's hat a breeze had blown away. I stretched out a hand – but he recovered his feet much frightened. He might have rolled a good way down the slope among the trees. At right cows & cow bells – The mountains covered with snow. Very fine sight. Hot with walking – yet close to Snow. I took some in my hand & swallowed it. Returned to Lauterbrunnen for carriage (gone round)   Lovely drive back to Interlaken

24. Thursday. On the lake of Thun Mountains green & wooded all round   Exquisite lake – slopes cultivated – vines chiefly – high up on their sticks – (vines everywhere in Switzerland. Drank the wine at Lunch & Dinners

(Nice hotel (with fresco. Paper figures on [*word missing*][86] of stairs) at Interlaken. Sorry to leave Interlaken

25. Came to Lausanne. Hôtel Gibbon   In omnibus   Steep hills – long time coming up. Full of people. Dark Salon à manger   Post Office building – Shutters to our window. No blinds. Very high up, looking down on tops of trees & houses, the lake beyond. The mountains behind – green

Went to Chillon. By water on the lake of Geneva – blue – clear. Got first down to Ouchy – the port by funicular rail. Fine view, though rather misty of the mountains on the right. Stopped at every little village or town till we reached Territet. The port for Chillon. Train to Chillon.

Young beautiful gaily attired woman showed us the Castle. Spoke German to the other couple – English to us – a coquettish manner. The castle quite astonishing – size – solidity – preservation   Were shown – Bonnivard's prison (a large vaulted place) – his pillar – near a window once divided off from the many other windows. Names. Byron   George Sand & other on pillar – iron rings   Were shown the beam on which the prisoners were hung. The hole through which they were thrown into the lake we saw through trap doors – horrible prisons – & the Oubliettes – (no fourth step) Returned by train through Clarens "sweet Clarens"   which we had also seen from lake – Had tea at Vevey. Verandah of hotel – (I liked up stairs)   Looked down on lake & road, & trees etc. Sunny & pretty.

26. Stayed on at Lausanne.

27. June[87]
Sunday at Lausanne. Went down to Ouchy – hot – sat under trees (see sketch) making a new harbour there. The Lac lovely – had some thunder before Inquired for Byron's room – shown an ordinary one. Had lunch in an ordinary salon of the hotel. Common place affair

28. Went to Zermatt – lunched in train.

29. Went up the Riffel-Alp. On a mule Very steep. Sudden turns up loose rocky stony ways. Mule's hind feet slipping Guide leading him by hand – Guide did not understand French. Only patois   A station being constructed for the Rack & Pinion R[ailwa]y – Italian workmen   A tremendous long distance   Steep zigzag over precipices. Wished I had not come – charge $8\frac{1}{2}$ francs – Hotel grandly situated as high as opposite Matterhorn –.

The snow limit. T.H. far behind walking
Immense hotel – & space round – Every
appliance – all brought up on Mule's back.
Met a number of them – Continual traffic
Old gentleman lost two days before & never
found[88] – Many ladies up there   I waited for
Tom – he toiled up on foot. Had lunch. Called
guide   Returned. Waited & rested about an
hour   Mounted, then got off a little way
down – walking alone – the guide gone on.
Felt a little alarm. A knot of rough workmen
seemed quarrelling. I passed through them
safely, met several men & mules   Difficult
descent, terrible slopes to look down upon.
Lovely trees & alpine roses. (A sort of rhodo-
dendron shrub)   Mounted again & scrambled back. A small dirty native woman in
front on a mule. The men laughing at her &
with her – Got back safely, & became used to
it. The [*word missing*?][86]

had a rail to keep up one's back –
The Matterhorn – near – grand – (see sketches)

30. Fine day – At Zermatt – Very ugly &
very old ladies with a general at table
Sellier's hotels at Zermatt all of them

Wonderful place – real dirty chalets   Very
brown faces, & clothes – dirty all – people &
streets & house – but picturesque   The Visp
boiling through the village   I went up the
stairs of a new chalet – Band played in evening
– outside Hotel. Matterhorn from bedroom
window – T.H. talked of Whymper[89] – he
knows him –

July 1. T.H. not well[90] – lunched by myself –
at Geneva. First Hotel. (Not good.) Got
medicine, (oil) for T.H. Left Hotel & went
Grand Hôtel du Paix near the Lac. Very fine.
(Musical box splendid. Geneva a great place
for them –) Fine view of Lake. Fine weather –
T.H. better – we walked out. I went out by
self in evening to bridge

2nd. Walked about Geneva – A wedding at
Cathedral – Geneva with gay ladies about

July 3. I went to Plain Palais Cemetery & found my ancestor's grave. Sir H. Davy[91] – grandmama's cousin I think. Also Calvin's Stone – very small. A canopy over pulpit

4 – Left Geneva for Dijon & Paris after lunching in train at Culoz – saw the debris of landslip across railway with trees & rocks upturned & rooted, & the torn side of the mountain perhaps an avalanche. No snow however.

Came again to Dijon – Saw 4 Cathedrals One very old – One called Saint-Bénigne Benign – a finely decorated carved & figured doorway – with obliterated [SKETCH] stones in porch. Fine church

5. Went to Paris – First went to Neuilly – Gordon[92] had left Tuesday previous – Saw the sister of Prop: A great fair along Neuilly   I hot & tired. Went to the Louvre – Had lunch with T.H. in Duval Restaurant

6. Went to Havre. Slept on the Alma. Rather rough night – but "wind be still" was the order of it –

7. Returned to Max Gate.

Saw in Louvre statue of highest court Functionary Period Saite a highly pleased expression [SKETCH] Egyptian mouth also a tomb with weeping cowled monks – 8 of 'em

Notes

The following works are quoted in the notes below by abbreviated titles as indicated in square brackets:

Gibson, James (ed), *The Complete Poems of Thomas Hardy* (Macmillan 1976) [*Complete Poems*].

Hardy, Evelyn and Robert Gittings (eds), *Some Recollections by Emma Hardy* (OUP 1961, rev. ed. 1979) [*Some Recollections*].

Hardy, Evelyn and F.B. Pinion (eds), *One Rare Fair Woman: Thomas Hardy's Letters to Florence Henniker 1893–1922* (Macmillan 1972) [*One Rare Fair Woman*].

Hardy, Florence Emily, *The Life of Thomas Hardy* (Macmillan 1962) [*Life*]. [It is now accepted that this is Hardy's own "disguised autobiography", deliberately written by him in the third person.]

Millgate, Michael, *Thomas Hardy: A Biography* (OUP, 1982).

Purdy, R.L. and Michael Millgate (eds), *The Collected Letters of Thomas Hardy*, Vol. I: 1840–1892 (OUP 1978) [*Collected Letters*].

Taylor, Richard H. (ed), *The Personal Notebooks of Thomas Hardy* (Macmillan 1978) [*Personal Notebooks*].

1   Emma was staying with her younger brother, Walter Gifford, at this address. (When Walter died in 1898 the Hardys took his children Gordon and Lilian into Max Gate, where they lived for several years.) Emma and Thomas Hardy were married at St Peter's Church, Elgin Avenue, Paddington, by Emma's uncle, Dr E. Hamilton Gifford, then Canon of Worcester and later Archdeacon of London. Emma later recalled her wedding day: "The day we were married was a perfect September day – 17th, 1874 – not a brilliant sunshine, but wearing a soft, sunny luminousness; just as it should be" (*Some Recollections*, p. 37).

2   Robert Gittings suggests that the deletion reads "Palace Hotel, Queensway", where the Hardys spent their wedding night.

3   The Hardys stayed at D. Morton's Family and Commercial Hotel, Queen's Road, Brighton. On this day Hardy wrote to his brother Henry: "I write a line to tell you all at home that the wedding took place yesterday, & that we are got as far as this on our way to Normandy & Paris. There were only Emma & I, her uncle who married us, & her brother, my landlady's daughter signed the book as one witness" (*Collected Letters*, I, p. 31). He added: "I am going to Paris for materials for my next story", as if this, rather than his honeymoon, was his primary purpose.

4   Emma's memory must have played her false: the fish she saw was probably a gurnard, which has separate rays on the leading edge of the pectoral fin, which it uses like "legs" to walk along the sea bed. I am indebted for this information to Mr P.S. Davis, Deputy Curator of the Hancock Museum, Newcastle.

5   Hardy exploited his experience of visiting Rouen in *The Hand of Ethelberta*, which he began writing at the end of the year.

6   Hardy noted in his copy of Murray's *Handbook of Visitors to Paris*, which he had brought to guide them, that this was "of every colour – marble walls & all"; cf. the description of Lord Mountclere's mansion in *The Hand of Ethelberta*.

7   Sir Sidney Smith (1764–1840), famous seaman.

8   The theologian Peter Abelard (1079–1142) and Héloïse (b. 1100), with whom he famously fell in love and secretly married. Their ashes were taken to Paris in 1800 and buried in 1817 in one sepulchre at Père la Chaise.

9   Honoré de Balzac (1799–1850), novelist.

10   Emma's sister Helen had married the Rev. Caddell Holder in 1869, in which year Emma went to live with them at the rectory in St Juliot, Cornwall.

11   The Hardys had not rented accommodation in which to live on their return from their honeymoon so they were now seeking suitable lodgings in south-west London.

12   Emma may have been toying with ideas for a story deriving from the appearance of the lady described in the previous entry.

13   The Hardys rented rooms at St David's Villa, Hook Road, Surbiton, where they stayed until March 1875. Emma's father, John Attersoll Gifford, had not been present at the wedding; as he was antagonistic to Hardy, it is not clear why he visited on this occasion. Gifford (1808–90) was a solicitor obliged to retire early because of his heavy drinking and thereafter supported by his mother's income until her death in 1860, when the division of her money forced the Giffords to live more modestly in Bodmin.

14   During their stay in Surbiton, Hardy's *Far from the Madding Crowd* had been published on 23 November 1874, and Hardy recorded that they saw "during their journeys to and from London, ladies carrying about copies of it" (*Life*, p. 101). He was now writing *The Hand of Ethelberta* and in early March 1875 had written to the publisher George Smith: "We are coming to Town for three months on account of Ethelberta, some London scenes occurring in her chequered career which I want to do as vigorously as possible – having already visited Rouen and Paris with the same object, other adventures of his taking place there" (*Collected Letters*, I, p. 35). The Hardys moved to Westbourne Grove on 19 March, with "their entire worldly goods" in four packing cases, and spent three months there following "an ordinary round of museum, theatre and concert-going, with some dining-out" (*Life*, p. 103).

15   The Hardys decided to move back to Dorset for practical reasons. Hardy had unsuccessfully house-hunted there in June but now they spent three nights in Bournemouth before going to Swanage.

16   St Swithin's Day. According to Hardy's poem, 'We Sat at the Window' (dated "Bournemouth, 1875"), the Hardys sat disconsolately watching the rain:
      We were irked by the scene, by our own selves; yes,
      For I did not know, nor did she infer
      How much there was to read and guess
      By her in me, and to see and crown
         By me in her.
      Wasted were two souls in their prime,
      And great was the waste, that July time
         When the rain came down.
Later in the day they took the steamer to Swanage.

17   The Hardys "found lodgings at the house of an invalided captain of smacks and ketches" [Captain Joseph Masters] (*Life*, p. 107). Here they

remained for ten months and Hardy completed *The Hand of Ethelberta*. In the novel, Swanage is called "Knollsea", West End Cottage furnishes the setting for Ethelberta's lodgings, and Captain Masters appears as Captain Flower.

18 Captain Joseph Masters (see note 17).

19 This paragraph and the succeeding passages seem to be preliminary sketches and local notes for an unpublished novella which she wrote at this time, entitled "The Maid on the Shore".

20 Hardy's sisters Mary (1841–1915) and Kate (1856–1940) visited Hardy and Emma for two weeks. Mary accompanied them on this steamer trip, of which her sketches survive.

21 On this occasion Hardy, his sisters and Emma were joined by Hardy's brother, Henry (1851–1928). The visit to Corfe formed the basis of Ethelberta's expedition to Corfe Castle with the historical society in *The Hand of Ethelberta*, chapter 31.

22 Hardy's own account of this journey is recorded in *Life*, pp. 110–111. In March 1876 the Hardys had left West End Cottage, Swanage, and taken lodgings in Yeovil. In May they spent two weeks in London prior to setting out for Holland.

23 Hardy writes that, visiting Holland, the first thing that struck them was that " 'the Dutch seemed like police perpetually keeping back an unruly crowd composed of waves' " (*Life*, p. 110).

24 In the diary, this underlined addition is written on the previous page to the left margin and under the rule below the sketch and caption.

25 Hardy's 36th birthday.

26 In Cologne, Hardy writes, he "was disappointed by the machine-made Gothic of the Cathedral" (*Life*, p. 110).

27 Hardy writes that in Maintz "they were impressed by a huge confirmation in the cathedral which, by the way, was accompanied by a tune like that of Keble's evening hymn" (*Life*, p. 110).

28 Hardy writes: "Heidelberg they loved, and looking west one evening from the top of the tower on the Königsstuhl, Hardy remarks on a singular optical effect that was almost tragic. Owing to mist the wide landscape itself was not visible, but 'the Rhine glared like a riband of blood, as if it serpentined through the atmosphere above the earth's surface' " (*Life*, p. 110).

29 From Heidelberg, Hardy records, "they went to Carlsruhe, where they attended a fair, and searched for a German lady Hardy had known in England, but were unable to find her" (*Life*, p. 110).

30 Hardy writes, in a passage deleted from the published version of the *Life*, that at Strasbourg "Mrs. Hardy was laid up, (probably by excessive walking). A thick brown mysterious fluid which her husband obtained at an Italian apothecary's and could never afterwards identify, set her right in a day or two" (*Personal Notebooks*, p. 221).

31 Kirland Manor in Cornwall, which the Gifford family rented from 1860 (when Emma was 20). Emma describes Kirland in *Some Recollections*, pp. 22–23.

32 "Here Hardy – maybe with his mind on *The Dynasts* – explored the field of Waterloo" (*Life*, p. 110). The Napoleonic wars had long held great fascination for Hardy because of childhood reading and family associations, so the exploration of Waterloo was a major event for him, if less so for his fatigued wife.

33 Michael Millgate records that "on the endpapers of his Baedeker for Holland and Belgium, [Hardy] drew a 'Plan of Hougomont – Sketched on the spot by T.H.' " (*Thomas Hardy: A Biography*, p. 183).

34   Hardy writes that he "spent some time in investigating the problem of the actual scene of the Duchess of Richmond's Ball, with no result that satisfied him, writing a letter while here to some London paper to that effect – a letter which has not been traced" (*Life*, p. 110).

35   A poignant entry since the Hardys had, Hardy says, received hints from relatives that they "appeared to be wandering about like two tramps" (*Life*, p. 111).

36   Here, Hardy says, "in the private parlour of 'The Turk's Head', over glasses of grog, the battle was fought yet again by the dwindling number of pensioners who had taken part in it" (*Life*, p. 111).

37   Possibly the publisher George Bentley (1828–95).

38   Hardy recalls "having a miserable passage on a windy night in a small steamer with cattle on board" (*Life*, p. 111).

39   Hardy and Emma stayed at Riverside Villa until 18 March 1878, which he later described as the "End of the Sturminster Newton idyll . . . Our happiest time" (*Life*, p. 118).

40   Wife of a local solicitor and landowner.

41   Mr Warry was another landowner. A gruesome anecdote of his, about a friend's tenant farmer sticking black thorns into the hearts of calves that died and then hanging the hearts on the crossbar of his chimney to prevent spreading the disease that had killed the calf, is found in *Life*, p. 112.

42   On 4 February 1887 Hardy finished writing *The Woodlanders*. "Having now some leisure, and the spring drawing near, Hardy carried into effect an idea that he had long entertained," Hardy writes (*Life*, p. 186), and left for Italy the day before Macmillan published the novel.

43   "The month had been mild hitherto, but no sooner had they started than the weather turned to snow; and a snowstorm persistently accompanied them across the Channel and southward beyond" (*Life*, p. 187).

44   "They broke the journey at Aix-les-Bains, at which place they arrived past midnight, and the snow being by this time deep a path was cleared with spades for them to the fly in waiting, which two horses, added by men turning the wheels, dragged with difficulty up the hill to the Hôtel Château Durieux – an old fashioned place with stone floors and wide fireplaces" (*Life*, p. 187).

45   17 March 1887.

46   "They were the only people there – the first visitors of the season – and in spite of a huge fire in their bedroom they found the next morning a cone of snow within each casement, and a snow film on the floor sufficient to show their tracks in moving about" (*Life*, p. 187).

47   "Hardy used to speak of a curious atmospheric effect they witnessed: he was surprised that the windows of the room they occupied – one of the best – should command the view of a commonplace paddock only, with a few broken rails and sheds. But presently 'what had seemed like the sky evolved a scene which uncurtained itself high up in the midst of the aerial expanse, as in a magic lantern, and vast mountains appeared there, tantalizingly withdrawing again as if they had been a mere illusion.'
    They stayed here a day or two, 'the mountains showing again coquettish signs of uncovering themselves, and again coquettishly pulling down their veil' " (*Life*, p. 187).

48   "Genoa, concerning the first aspect of which from the train Hardy wrote a long time after the lines entitled 'Genoa and the Mediterranean', though that city – so pre-eminently the city of marble – 'everything marble', he writes, 'even little doorways in slums' – nobly redeemed its character when they visited its palaces during their stay" (*Life*, p. 187). In the poem Hardy records his first view of "multimarbled Genova the Proud/ . . . not as the Beauty but the Dowd", yet later "Palazzo Doria's

orange bowers/ Went far to mend these marrings of thy soul-subliming powers" (*Complete Poems*, p. 100).

49   Lucy Baxter (1837–1902) was the married daughter of the Dorset poet William Barnes (1800–86), who died the previous year. Mrs Baxter wrote, under the pseudonym 'Leader Scott', much on Italian themes. Hardy had known Mrs Baxter since she was a girl.

50   Mrs Baxter had obtained lodgings for the Hardys at the Villa Trollope in the Piazza dell'Indipidenza, where they stayed throughout their visit to Florence. Anthony Trollope (1815–82) had written *Doctor Thorne* in the house, which was then owned by his family. His mother settled in Florence in 1843.

51   Michael Millgate notes that at the Pitti Palace Hardy jotted down in his Baedeker brief notes on several works, "and observed of Titian's Magdalene that the artist had been interested only in painting a handsome woman" (*Thomas Hardy: A Biography*, p. 281).

52   "At Pisa . . . they stood at the top of the leaning tower during a peal of the bells, which shook it under their feet, and saw the sun set from one of the bridges over the Arno, as Shelley had probably seen it from the same bridge many a time" (*Life*, p. 188).

53   (Sir) Edmund Gosse (1849–1928), man of letters, was for many years a close friend of Hardy.

54   Hardy devoted several pages of the *Life* (pp. 188–91) to describing their stay in Rome.

55   After the discomforts of the Hotel Bologna, the Hardys settled at the Hotel d'Allemagne in the Via Condotti, a street opposite "the steps descending from the church of SS. Trinità dei Monti, on the south side of which stands the house where Keats died. Hardy liked to watch of an evening . . . the house hard by, in which no mind could conjecture what had been lost to English literature in the early part of the same century" (*Life*, p. 188).

56   "There was a great spurt of building going on at this time, on which [Hardy] remarks, 'I wonder how anybody can have any zest to erect a new building in Rome, in the overpowering presence of decay on the mangy and rotting walls of old erections, originally of fifty times the strength of the new'" (*Life*, p. 189). This thought inspired Hardy's sonnet, 'Rome: Building a New Street in the Ancient Quarter/(April 1887)': "And yet within these ruins' very shade/The singing workmen shape and set and join/Their frail new mansion's stuccoed cove and quoin/With no apparent sense that years abrade" (*Complete Poems*, p. 103). This theme is also reflected in a 31 March letter to Edmund Gosse (*Collected Letters*, I, p. 163).

57   Hardy's second wife, Florence, deleted from the typescript of the *Life* Hardy's own generous account of Emma's courage on this occasion. It is included in full in the *Personal Notebooks* (p. 227): "Two or three slightly unpleasant occurrences chequered their stay in Rome, but were not of serious moment. One was that when Hardy was descending the Via di Aracoeli, carrying a small old painting he had just bought in a slum at the back of the Capitoline Hill, three men prepared to close on him as if to rob him, apparently mistaking him for a wealthy man owing to his wearing a fur-edged coat. They could see that both his hands were occupied in holding the picture, but what they seemed not to be perceiving was that he was not alone, Mrs Hardy being on the opposite of the narrow way. She cried out to her husband to be aware, and with her usual courage rushed across to the back of the men, who disappeared as if by magic."

58   The Hardys' 31 March 1887 visit to the graves of the poets John Keats and Percy Bysshe Shelley in the Protestant cemetery inspired his poem 'Rome/At the Pyramid of Cestius near the Graves of Shelley and Keats/ (1887).' The tomb of the unknown Caius Cestius, who died within thirty years before Christ, inspires Hardy's humorous "Who, then, was Cestius, /

And what is he to me?", and his conclusion that Cestius's belated fame is in fact simply reflected from his interment near Keats and Shelley, "two immortal Shades" (*Complete Poems*, pp. 104–5). On the day of this visit Hardy sent Edmund Gosse "a violet or two" from Keats's grave: "He is covered with violets in full bloom just now, & thousands of daisies stud the grass around" (*Collected Letters*, I, p. 163).

59   The inscription on Keats's grave is: "This Grave contains all that was Mortal of a Young English Poet – who on his death-bed – in the bitterness of his heart – at the malicious power of his enemies – desired these words to be engraven on his Tomb Stone/'Here lies one whose name was writ in Water'."

60   Edmund Gosse had written on 22 March thanking Hardy for *The Woodlanders*, promising to review it and speculating on the "original" for Little Hintock. Hardy identified this as Melbury Osmond in his 31 March reply, but on 5 April wrote from Florence saying that he had meant to say that this was the source of *Great* Hintock (*Collected Letters*, I, pp. 163–4).

61   On this day Hardy wrote to his mother Jemima (1813–1904), saying that "We went to-day along the Appian Way towards the Three Taverns, the road by which St Paul came into Rome, as described in the last Chapter of Acts" (*Collected Letters*, I, p. 163). Here he "was obsessed by a vision of a chained file of prisoners plodding wearily along towards Rome, one of the most haggard of whom was to be famous through the ages as the founder of Pauline Christianity" (*Life*, p. 189).

62   Daniel O'Connell (1775–1847).

63   Hardy noted: "'The monk who showed us the hole in which stood Saint Peter's Cross in the Church of S. Pietro in Montorio, and fetched up a pinch of clean sand from it, implying it had been there ever since the apostle's crucifixion, was a man of cynical humour, and gave me an indescribably funny glance from the tail of his eye as if to say: "You see well enough what an imposture it all is!" . . . Perhaps there is something in my appearance which makes [these Roman monks] think me a humorist also'" (*Life*, p. 189).

64   They returned to the Villa Trollope. "Returning to Florence on 'a soft green misty evening following rain', [Hardy] found the scenery soothing after the gauntness of Rome" (*Life*, p. 191).

65   Florence Hardy deleted Hardy's recollection of this from the published version of the *Life:* "Another risk, of which however they were not conscious at the moment, was one incurred by herself, who in her eagerness for exploration lingered for rather a long time in the underground dens of the Coliseum. An attack of malaria in a mild form followed, which went off in a few days; but with, to them, the singular result that at the same date in spring for three or four years afterwards the same feverishness returned, in decreasing strength, till it finally left off appearing" (*Personal Notebooks*, p. 227).

66   Possibly **Mrs Craik** (Dinah Mulock, 1826–87), authoress of *John Halifax, Gentleman* (1857).

67   Elizabeth Barrett Browning (1806–1861), poetess and wife of Robert Browning.

68   Violet Paget (1856–1935), who lived in Florence and wrote under the pseudonym 'Vernon Lee'. Her half-brother, Eugene Lee-Hamilton, was disabled.

69   Hardy records that he "found more pleasure in Venice than in any Italian city previously visited, in spite of bad weather during a part of his stay there", and devotes pp. 192–5 of the *Life* to an account of their stay.

70   "The bell of the Campanile of S. Marco strikes the hour," Hardy notes with an unexpected comparison, "and its sound has exactly that tin-tray

timbre given out by the bells of Longpuddle and Weatherbury, showing that they are of precisely the same-proportioned alloy'' (*Life*, p. 193).

71 Hardy's thoughts on visiting the Doge's Palace are found in the *Life*, pp. 192–4.

72 The Hardys "were most kindly received and entertained during their brief stay by friends to whom they had introductions" (*Life*, p. 194). Mrs Arthur Bronson enjoyed a warm friendship, at her home (La Mura) built into the city walls, with Robert Browning and Henry James, who wrote an introduction to her account of Browning in Venice. While the Hardys were there, "Mrs Bronson showed them many things" (*Life*, p. 194).

73 Mrs Daniel Curtis, another (American) friend of Robert Browning and Henry James. The Bronsons and the Curtises held prominent literary and social gatherings.

74 Hardy writes that "she was a great beauty, having the well-defined hues and contours of foreigners in the South ... When asked afterwards how she was dressed, he said in a green velvet jacket with fluffy tags, a grey hat and feathers, a white veil with seed pearls, and a light figured skirt of a yellowish colour. She had a charming manner, her mind flying from one subject to another like a child's as she spoke her pretty attempts at English. 'But I lie-eek moch to do it!' ... 'Si, si!' ... 'Oh noh, noh!' ... It is not known whether the Italian Contessa in *A Group of Noble Dames* was suggested by her; but there are resemblances" (*Life*, pp. 194–5).

75 22 April 1887.

76 Hardy's notes on the cathedral are found in the *Life*, p. 195, and "It was while here on the roof, he thought in after years, though he was not quite sure, that he conceived the Milan Cathedral scene in *The Dynasts*."

77 Hardy was interested in 'The Bridge of Lodi', an old French tune. Having met the young Scottish lieutenant, mentioned in Emma's previous paragraph and described by Hardy as "apparently a sort of Farfrae", and enthused him about the Napoleonic battle which inspired the tune, Hardy visited the bridge with his young companion: "Over the quiet flowing of the Adda the two re-enacted the fight, and the 'Little Corporal's' dramatic victory over the Austrians" (*Life*, p. 196). Hardy later recalled this in the poem 'The Bridge of Lodi / (Spring 1887)' (*Complete Poems*, pp. 107–9).

78 Her brother-in-law, Henry Hardy.

79 Hardy remarked on "the vying of 'the young greens with the old greens, the greens of yesterday and the greens of yesteryear'" at Como (*Life*, p. 196).

80 A sentiment shared by Emma's husband: "The cheerful scenes of life and gaiety here after the poetical decay of Venice came as the greatest possible contrast, and a not unwelcome change" (*Life*, p. 195).

81 Hardy says that "It was too early in the year for Lucerne, and they stayed there only a day" (*Life*, p. 196).

82 Hardy says that they started for Switzerland to escape "the racket of the coming Diamond Jubilee" (*Life*, p. 292). Because of the Jubilee, the Channel steamer was almost empty, and their journey progressed with great ease.

83 Diamond Jubilee day: "they celebrated it by attending a Jubilee Concert in the Cathedral" (*Life*, p. 292).

84 "At Interlaken the comparative solitude was just as refreshing, the rosy glow from the Jungfrau, visible at three in the morning from Hardy's bedroom, seeming an exhibition got up for themselves alone; and a pathetic procession of empty omnibuses went daily to and from each railway train between shops that looked like a banquet spread for people who delayed to come" (*Life*, p. 292). A further note of Hardy's records: "It was either in the train as it approached Interlaken, or while he was there looking at the peak,

that there passed through his mind the sentiments afterwards expressed in the lines called 'The Schreckhorn: with thoughts of Leslie Stephen'" (*Life*, p. 293). The poem, admired by Stephen's daughter, Virginia Woolf, is in *Complete Poems*, p. 322.

85   Hardy recalls that here they were "overlooking the scene of *Manfred* – where a baby had just been born" (*Life*, p. 292).

86   The diary has been resewn at some time resulting in the obscuring of the text.

87   The Hotel Gibbon was named after the famous historian Edward Gibbon (1737–94), author of *Decline and Fall of the Roman Empire*. On this date, though Emma does not record the fact, Hardy recalled Gibbon's *Autobiography*, which tells that between 11.0 p.m. and midnight on 27 June 1787 Gibbon wrote the last lines of his masterwork. Between the same hours 110 years later, Hardy now sat in Gibbon's garden, and this inspired his poem, 'Lausanne / In Gibbon's Old Garden: 11–12 p.m.' (*Complete Poems*, pp. 105–6).

88   Having set Emma on the pony, Hardy "slowly searched all the way down the track for some clue to the missing man, afterwards writing a brief letter to *The Times* to say there was no sign visible of foul play anywhere on the road" (*Life*, p. 294). The missing man was called James Robert Cooper.

89   Hardy was inspired by the view of the Matterhorn, and the recollection of a climbing accident on 14 July 1865 when seven men became the first to reach its summit before four of them fell to death on the way down, to begin a sonnet, finished later, entitled 'Zermatt / To the Matterhorn / (June–July 1897)' (*Complete Poems*, p. 106). Edward Whymper (1840–1911) was the only Englishman to survive, and Hardy had met him in 1894 (see *Life*, p. 264).

90   Hardy suffered heat exhaustion after climbing up the mountain path two days earlier. He told Florence Henniker in a letter on 3 July that he was "pulled down a little, Em being in excellent health and vigour" (*One Rare Fair Woman*, p. 65). While recuperating in the Hotel de la Paix he "had a curious sense of impending tragedy" (*Personal Notebooks*, p. 248), which was later realised in the murder by an Italian anarchist of an Austrian Empress, whose early beauty had inspired some verses and almost inspired Hardy also to write a novel about her.

91   Sir Humphry Davy (1778–1829) was inventor of the safety-lamp. While Emma was on this expedition, Hardy was writing from the hotel to Florence Henniker: "The windows here command a full view of the Lake, and the haunts of the poets; also of the 'arrowy Rhone' (Byron is literally true in what he says of 'Lake Leman' (Geneva) in *Childe Harold*. Yet what is the use of coming to such places for association's sake? Those who write rapturously about them from Rousseau onwards care nothing about them *now*" (*One Rare Fair Woman*, p. 65). The sentiment is echoed in a contemporary note: "These haunts of the illustrious! Ah, but *they* are gone now, and care for their chosen nooks no more!" (*Life*, p. 295).

92   Emma's nephew Gordon Gifford (see note 1), who had been improving his French at a school in Paris.